Josephine Butler
Her Work and Principles,
and their meaning for the Twentieth Century.

Especially written for the Josephine Butler Centenary 1828-1928

Millicent G. Fawcett G.B.E

and

E. M. Turner

Facsimile reprint 2002: First published 1927

Published by Portrayer Publishers

For information on any of our books, please contact:
Portrayer Publishers, 55 Red Lane, Hill Cliffe, Appleton, Warrington, CHESHIRE, Unit
Kingdom, WA4 5AL.

Telephone: 44 (0) 1925 497783

Facsimile: 44 (0) 1925 497783

e-mail us at : publishing@portrayer.co.uk

ISBN: 0954263286

A catalogue record for this book is available from the British Library

Produced in the United Kingdom by Bookchase Ltd (London)

ver Illustration: Mike Barlow-Portrayer Publishers.

JOSEPHINE BUTLER

*Her Work and Principles, and their
meaning for the Twentieth Century*

Specially written for the Josephine Butler Centenary, 1828-1928

BY

MILLICENT G. FAWCETT, G.B.E.

AND

E. M. TURNER

Our claim was no claim of women's rights only ; it was larger and
deeper ; it was a claim for the rights of all—all men and women—to the
respect in their persons of the great principles of Justice and Equality
and Liberty.—*Josephine Butler*.

The evidence which truth carries with it is superior to all argument ;
it neither wants the support nor dreads the opposition of the greatest
abilities.—*Lord Chatham*.

THE ASSOCIATION FOR MORAL & SOCIAL HYGIENE,
ORCHARD HOUSE, GREAT SMITH STREET,
LONDON, S.W. 1.

1927.

PRICE 2/6.

Quotations from Mrs. Butler, used by me in preparing this book, are in the main taken direct from the works indicated ; but some have been taken from *Josephine Butler : an Autobiographical Memoir by G. W. and L. A. Johnson.* These have been gratefully marked by me with the initials J.J. I have found this book most valuable from every point of view and not least so for its excellent index.

Printed by H. R. Grubb, Ltd., Croydon.

CONTENTS.

CHIEF DATES IN JOSEPHINE BUTLER'S LIFE.

1828   Birth at Milfield Hill, Northumberland.

1852   Marriage with George Butler.

1852-56 Life at Oxford.

1864   Sudden death of her little daughter at Cheltenham.

Parliament passes the first Contagious Diseases Act.

1866   Life at Liverpool.
Amended Contagious Diseases Act passed.

1868   Death of John Grey of Dilston.

1869   Last Contagious Diseases Act passed.

Founding of The Ladies' National Association and the National Association for the Repeal of the C. D. Acts now the Association for Moral and Social Hygiene).

The " Ladies' Appeal and Protest " against the C. D. Acts.

1870	The Colchester Election.
1871	Royal Commission on the Operation of the C. D. Acts.
1875	The International Abolitionist Federation founded at Geneva.
1880-81	Select Committee of the House of Commons appointed to report on the C. D. Acts.
1881	Licensed Houses closed in Colmar, Alsace.
1882	Life at Winchester.
1883	Suspension of the Contagious Diseases Acts in Great Britain.
1886	Total Repeal of the Contagious Diseases Acts.
	Regulation of Prostitution abolished in Norway.
1890	Death of Canon Butler.
1895	Mrs. Butler accorded a public reception by the Mayor at Colmar ; the first European town to abolish licensed houses.
1901	Licensed houses closed in Denmark.
1906	The " Police des Moeurs " abolished in Denmark.
1906	Death of Josephine Butler.

The Life and Work of

The following events which have happened since her death are directly due to the work initiated by Josephine Butler and her Abolitionist colleagues.

1911   Regulation abolished in Bulgaria. Licensed houses closed in Holland and Serbia.

1913   Appointment of British Royal Commission on Venereal Diseases in England. The Regulationist " Police des Moeurs " abolished in Holland.

1916   Royal Commission Report on Venereal Diseases completely endorses Abolitionist principles.

1918   Regulation abolished in Sweden. The " tolerated houses " closed in Indian Cantonments by order of Commander-in-Chief.

1921   Tolerated houses and segregated areas closed in Burma. Licensed houses closed in Vienna.

1922   Regulation abolished in Gibraltar, Poland, and the Czechoslovak Republic.

1923   The A.M.S.H. publish draft bill (the Public Places (Order) Bill) to repeal the Solicitation Laws in England.

1925   First Report of the Colonial Office Advisory Committee on Social Hygiene.

The International Abolitionist Federation celebrates its Jubilee at Geneva. Geneva closes all licensed houses and thus completes abolition throughout Switzerland.

1925   The Public Places (Order) Bill introduced into the House of Commons by Lady Astor, M.P., and in the House of Lords by the Lord Balfour of Burleigh. (1926).

1927   The licensed houses closed in Strasbourg, Hamburg, Leipzig, and Gratz.

The Report of the Experts' Committee of the League of Nations on the Traffic in Women and Children completely justifies Mrs. Butler's condemnation of licensed houses and the Regulation system.

Regulation abolished in Germany.

The licensed houses closed in Mulhouse, Alsace.

Licensed houses closed in the Rhineland.

The Government sets up a Committee to inquire into the operation of the Solicitation Laws in Great Britain.

CHAPTER I.

INTRODUCTORY.

"No men need to be slaves to bad laws who desire to be free ; no nation needs to submit to injustice or to bad government."—JOSEPHINE BUTLER.

THE more I dwell upon the details of Josephine Butler's life and work the more I become convinced that she should take the rank of the most distinguished Englishwoman of the nineteenth century. She created a movement which has continually progressed since her time. When she inaugurated it, she stood almost alone—quite alone if we omit her husband and other members of her family. Of course, this domestic support was of untold value to her personally, and enabled her gradually to create a personal following of men and women who had unbounded confidence in the soundness of her understanding and in her clear perception on all moral issues. To set against this, however, she was vehemently assailed by two, if not three powerful professions, and it is only since deeper research and wider knowledge have been obtained that it has gradually dawned upon ordinary men and women that the course she advocated was based on justice and commonsense, and has been continually reinforced by increasing knowledge and experience.

1

The Life and Work of

The Report issued in February, 1927, by the League of Nations on the Traffic in Women and Children, is a corroboration of everything which Josephine Butler stood for from the middle of the 19th century onwards. The wisdom and insight of the course she advocated are almost universally recognised, at any rate, in the English-speaking countries. If we endeavour to study the causes which made her what she was, it becomes clear that in nearly all the outward circumstances surrounding her she was peculiarly fortunate. She was never called upon to waste her strength of will and mind in combating domestic opposition. Nothing could have been more conducive to the fostering of her special gifts than her early home training, especially that received from her father. Moreover, for carrying through important international work, the Grey family, of which she was a member, afforded unusual facilities ; for she had near relatives, who were also devoted friends and colleagues, in several European countries. One brother-in-law, for instance, had settled in Italy, as a young man, and not only spoke Italian fluently, but had mastered many of its local dialects so perfectly that he was called upon officially in 1821 to act as interpreter of many of the Italian witnesses in the trial of Queen Caroline. Her marriage was equally fortunate. Her husband, George Butler, son of the Dean of Peterborough, was not only a brilliant scholar but a most remarkable man in every way. His intimate friend, John Anthony Froude, the historian, wrote of him in after life " as the most variously gifted man in body and mind that he ever knew." In her husband she found the keen sympathy of a fellow-worker ; her sons, in their turn, supported her especially in the development of her work in foreign countries. And besides these happy personal surroundings, many of which may of course be largely attributed to her own gracious and generous nature, the very time in which she lived was one in which the whole social atmosphere, as regards women's work and place in the world, was changing and improving, every decade giving to women greater scope to develop freely according to the gifts with which nature and education had endowed them. The whole attitude of mind of the general public in regard to women's work was gradually changing from an invariable and monotonous " No " into the more genial and expansive " Why not ? "

It is obvious that this change did not affect women only ; it affected the whole community : men and women of all classes ; but to women it was especially a time of an awakening out of repression into freedom ; doors were being opened ; barriers were being taken down, education was being reorganised and reformed. Thomas Campbell, the poet, for example, was helping to found University College, open to all sects and creeds without restriction. It was a time, too, when great literature was being written : literature in which women were taking an honourable part. Moreover, the end had come of the succession to the Crown of the undesirable sons of George III, and a fair young girl of pure instincts and uncommon strength of will sat on the throne of her ancestors. In a word, the Victorian age was the time of the Brontës,

of Mrs. Gaskell, of John Stuart Mill, of Mrs.
Browning, of Harriet Martineau, of Miss Herschell
and Mrs. Somerville ; and besides these there were
Dickens and Thackeray, Tennyson and Browning
and Hood, as well as Lord Shaftesbury with his
passion for helping the poor to a happier life ;
and there was Disraeli, with his novels helping
to shape the Young England Party with Lord
John Manners as one of its leaders ; and there
was Florence Nightingale standing for efficiency
and honesty as well as for humanity in the midst of
the ghastly muddle and waste of the Crimean War.*

All this time that the Social and Literary
Movement was progressing, there was also the
Political Movement claiming a fuller representation of the nation in Parliament, giving to workmen,
and later also to women, a share in determining
the national destiny.

In 1868 the Reform Bill of that year gave the
working class vote a strength and reality it had
never had before. The political genius of Disraeli
had wrested from the party to which he was opposed
the exclusive possession of the advocacy of a wide
extension of the franchise. He had " educated his
party " to some purpose when he secured for
them a share in the great work of extending the
political freedom which was then in the course of
being achieved. It was just at this time that the
political work to which Josephine Butler devoted
herself opened before her. She had for many years,
indeed ever since her early married life in Oxford,

*Prof. G. M. Trevelyan in his " History of the Nineteenth Century "
tells us that during the Crimean War " She brought down the death
rate " in the hospitals at Scutari from 42 per cent. to 22 per thousand.
p. 306.

given her best energies to the rescue and help of outcast women. The legislation known as the Contagious Diseases Acts had been hurriedly passed through Parliament without adequate discussion, in part even behind closed doors. There were three of these Acts, passed in 1864, 1866 and 1869. Their ostensible purpose was to stamp out in the Army and Navy the diseases associated with sexual immorality. But the Acts did not apply to men at all, but to women only. Their main feature was the compulsory detention in hospital with physical examination at frequently recurring intervals, of women *stated by the military police* to be prostitutes. These Acts were accompanied by no adequate safeguards against injustice, no hearing before a judge, no trial by jury, and no appeal ; they contained, in a word, the worst form of legalised injustice, and they placed in the hands of the police an instrument of cruel injustice such as no human being ought to be authorised to use.

To oppose these Acts, to bring about their repeal, Josephine Butler set before herself as the object of her life. It was to her an imperative call of duty which could not be mistaken. The Colchester Election in 1870, following hard upon the great extension of the franchise in 1868, (instituting household suffrage for men in the boroughs) gave her the most tremendous triumph that a woman has ever achieved in politics, and this was followed about a year later by an almost equally great triumph at another bye-election. The voice of the newly enfranchised electors was unmistakable. The Government, whether reluctant or not, was forced to listen to it.

The triumph of 1870 was repeated in **1883**. Another great extension of the franchise had been carried in 1880 granting Household Suffrage in the counties, and in these years Mrs. Butler secured another great victory, for the Acts were suspended in 1883 and totally repealed in 1886.

She never lived to see the enfranchisement of women, but if she had she would have recognised it as a still further strengthening of the foundations on which she had been building.

In Mr. and Mrs. Johnson's valuable book on Josephine Butler, a book to which I cannot too warmly express my obligations, they *rightly* give as its sub-title the words " An Autobiographical Memoir." I purposely emphasise the word "rightly" because it was unnecessary for them, and is unnecessary for any subsequent writer to add to what Mrs. Butler herself has written of her life, her work, and of her intimate and affectionate relations with her family and friends and with all who co-operated with her. She had the voice of a ready speaker ; " while I was musing the fire kindled, then spake I with my tongue," are words which seem to bring her very vividly to my remembrance ; but even more than the voice of the ready speaker, she had the pen of the ready writer. One is astonished when one comes to realise the great volume of her writings. The appendix to this memoir shows that she left behind her no fewer than thirty books, some of them periodicals to which for months and sometimes for years she was the principal contributor. Her books naturally vary in size and importance but they practically cover the whole of her public activities, and not a few deal with her most sacred personal memories; her devotion to her father and to her husband; her anguish and subsequent prostration caused by the sudden and tragic death of her only little daughter. Her *Memoir of John Grey of Dilston* tells us of the conditions of her early home life and training. Her *Recollections of George Butler* tells of her happy marriage, the life of the two together at Oxford, Cheltenham, Liverpool, and Winchester, while her *Personal Reminiscences of a Great Crusade* gives a thrilling narrative of a political struggle unique in its character and results. In using the material found in these, subsequent writers (of whom I am proud to be one) have no need to fear that they are disregarding Mrs. Butler's charge to her sons that they should allow no biography of herself to be written. In the memorandum she left on this subject she wrote :

" the part I have taken in the Abolitionist cause is sufficiently detailed in a book entitled *Personal Reminiscences of a Great Crusade* . . . That Crusade being, so to speak, public property, you cannot help notices being given of my part and your Father's in it . . . But beyond that, it is my desire that nothing personal should be brought before the public."

She added :

" It would seem to me an impertinence for anyone to wish to enquire into or write of my own personal or spiritual life and experiences."

It appears, therefore, to me, and I believe to all who had the honour of Mrs. Butler's friendship, that she has herself defined the limits within which we may work. We may use her published autobiographical books, but we may not try to raise the veil with which she has covered her inner spiritual experiences. The amount of autobiographical detail which she published during her life is so great that we can never complain of lack of material ; and besides this a wholly legitimate and very wide field of investigation is open to us, in tracing the immense difference already effected in the whole tone of society, in the Press, in Parliament, and in legislation on the subjects to which she devoted her life.

It is difficult, perhaps impossible, for anyone to picture to himself the vast change which has actually been accomplished, and it is a change for the good, a transition from a worse to a better state of society, of morals, of thought and of action. In this connection I may be pardoned if I quote from the late Rt. Hon. James Stuart's introduction to Mr. and Mrs. Johnson's book. It will be remembered that Mr. Stuart was one of Mrs. Butler's most ardent fellow-workers. As a young man, fresh from University honours, first at St. Andrew's and later at Trinity College, Cambridge, he joined her in her opposition to Sir Henry Storks, the Government Candidate in the Colchester Election of 1870, and with herself became the leading protagonist in the fight which quickly arose against the C. D. Acts of 1864, 1866 and 1869. Mrs. Butler had already had experience of Mr. Stuart's great powers as an organiser and worker in other and less hotly contested fields, *e.g.*, in providing higher education for women and the creation of that which was afterwards known as University Extension, so that no one outside her own family had more knowledge of her power and character than he had ; and he soon after her death in 1906, wrote of her thus :

"Josephine Butler was one of the great people of the world. In character, in work done, in influencing others, she was among those few great people who have moulded the course of things. The world is different because she lived . . . She was a great leader of men and women and a skilful and intrepid General in the battles she fought. As an orator she touched the hearts of her hearers as no one else has done to whom I have listened. She aimed at a perfectly definite object, but round that object there gathered in her mind many others, all converging to the same end. She left behind her wherever she went new thoughts and new aims and new ideals . . . She had to endure much, especially in the early years of her crusade—the averted glance of former friends —the brutal attacks of ignorant opponents—but the inspiration of a mighty purpose enabled her to rise above all that and to preserve a serenity of mind and of manner through it all. . . .

And now, what is the sum of it all ? It seems to me to be this, that we must all be glad that she lived. We are each of us individually better and the world as a whole is better, because she lived and the seed that she has sown can never die."

This fine tribute indicates what I hope will be the scope of this book. An attempt will be made to compare the *Then* with the *Now* ; to measure the lasting effect of Mrs. Butler's life's work and to tell how far her Standard has been carried and what the prospects are of further victories for the great cause of which she was the leading champion.

Note. After writing the foregoing I had the advantage of conversation with one of Mrs. Butler's grandchildren, Mr. A. S. G. Butler, the architect. He has a most vivid remembrance of her and spoke to me with enthusiasm of her marvellous personal charm, of her gifts as a musician, and as a linguist, and in amateur theatricals." About her speaking he corroborated what I have already quoted from James Stuart, that she had the power of moving the hearts of her hearers as few have done.

It was my misfortune that I never came into personal contact with Mrs. Butler until 1885 ; the occasion was our common interest in Mr. Stead's Crusade for the protection of children who were being, almost openly, sold in London for what the Royal Commission in 1871 had called "infamous purposes." This Commission had unanimously recommended the raising of the age of protection for little girls which was then fixed at 13 years ; notwithstanding this recommendation Parliament took no steps whatever towards carrying it out until Mr. Stead entered the lists and from the Parliamentary point of view carried everything before him. After then making Mrs. Butler's personal acquaintance and receiving the honour of her friendship, I never missed an opportunity of seeing her when she was in or near London.

Josephine Butler

CHAPTER II.

EARLY YEARS AND THEIR INFLUENCE.

"It only very gradually dawned with perfect clearness on my own mind, that it is the old inveterate, the deeply-rooted evil of prostitution itself against which we are destined to make war."—JOSEPHINE BUTLER.

READERS of Mrs. Butler's accounts of her work will be struck by the frequency with which she appeals to the main principles of the British Constitution, to Magna Carta, to the Bill of Rights, to the Habeas Corpus Statute and Trial by Jury. And she did not omit to point out that the elder Pitt when Lord Chatham, had referred to these as *the Bible of the British Constitution*.

The famous words of the Great Charter were often in her mind " To no man will we sell and to no man will we deny or delay right or justice "; " No freeman " as Green translates it, " shall be seized or imprisoned or dispossessed or outlawed or in any way brought to ruin ; we will not go against any man nor send against him, save by legal judgment of his peers or by the law of the land." These are great words, and they thrill us still. One copy, as J. R. Green* reminded us, still remains in the British Museum, injured by age and fire but with the royal seal still hanging from the brown and shrivelled parchment.

* *See* page 124, Green's " Short History of the English People."

It was on these great constitutional principles that the early education of Josephine Butler was founded. Her father had taken part, as a young man, in the struggle which preceded the passing of the Great Reform Bill of 1832 ; he was a free-trader when Waterloo was fought ; an ardent supporter of Clarkson and Wilberforce in their agitation against slavery ; and he brought up his children on the principles which had always guided his own conduct and opinions in public affairs.

John Grey of Dilston, born in 1785, was one of the most remarkable men of his generation ; his own father having died when the lad was only eight years old, he was very early placed in a position of responsibility which did not fail to make a life-long impression on his character. His mother, when he was still a mere child, used to speak of him as " my man, John," and well he deserved the title. Whilst very young in years, he became a leader in almost everything he undertook, and particularly was this the case in regard to agriculture. He found the system under which farms were cultivated in his native county, Northumberland, primitive almost to the point of savagery. He, by example as well as by precept, and aided by his kindly and generous neighbourliness, gradually brought about an immense improvement until the whole district became an example of good farming and high productiveness.

The Derwentwater estates, sequestrated in consequence of its former owner's part in the rebellion of 1715, had been by Act of Parliament granted to the Greenwich Hospital and were, therefore, used for the maintenance of Disabled Seamen of the Royal Navy. In 1833 Mr. Grey was appointed the manager of these estates, the revenue of which rose under his rule from £25,000 to £40,000 per annum. This represented no harshness, severity or rack-renting, but was the result of increased productiveness brought about by improved methods of farming and by the judicious application of capital to the soil.

Mr. Grey's position in his county made him the trusted friend of its chief inhabitants. Earl Grey, of Reform Bill fame, Sir George Grey of Falloden, Lord Durham, Lord Althorpe, and many others were his associates and friends not only in reference to agricultural affairs, but also in political matters of the first importance. He was familiarly known as " the Black Prince of the North "; and this had reference not only to his dark complexion and handsome countenance, but also to his authoritative manner and power of will and mind. He had a small estate of his own and this, his daughter felt, helped him to look at all questions regarding landlord and tenant from the double point of view.

Such was the man who had in hand the early training of Josephine Butler.

John Grey was an enthusiastic sportsman and a very straight rider; he accustomed all his children to the saddle as soon as they were old enough to sit on a pony; his eldest son was a quite celebrated rider and till quite late in life, Mrs. Butler was also a bold and skilful rider and all through her life a great lover of horses.

There were other formative influences at work

to make Josephine Grey what she afterwards became. She wrote of her father in after years : " He made us read Coke and Blackstone and impressed upon us from our childhood a horror of slavery and all arbitrary power. His own character and my mother's made us alive to great principles from early days." It should be noted that she inherited her love of freedom from her mother as well as from her father, for John Grey's wife was the descendant of a Huguenot family which had fled from France after the Revocation of the Edict of Nantes. Therefore, we are justified in saying of her that she was nobly born on both sides.

The very position of her home was such as to stimulate the mind of an imaginative child. It was near the Border, not far from Flodden, and it had, therefore, all the romantic traditions associated with the old Border warfare ; the forays, in expectation of which the cattle were driven into half fortified shelters ; the Peel towers, where watch was kept when the Scots raiders were expected ; all these things had a share in making Mrs. Butler what she afterwards became ; and we cannot help being reminded of another great woman whose childhood was also spent in a border country frequently disturbed by war. But there was this difference ; the border warfare between England and Scotland was, in Mrs. Butler's childhood, only a romantic memory, while in Joan's case it was a grim and ever-present reality ; her village was attacked by the Burgundians in the dead of the night and she and her little brothers and sisters were roused out of their beds to be

JOHN GREY
Of Milfield Hill, and of Dilston. Northumberland.

From a portrait by G. Patten, A.R.A., July, 1852.

taken to a place of safety. The difference was, of course, immense ; but the childish experiences of the two were alike in this that, they awoke in each, thoughts " beyond the reaches of their souls."

The education of Josephine Butler was not only what I have endeavoured to indicate ; it was also profoundly religious. Her father was a deeply religious man.   She recalls his reading of the Bible, especially of the prophet Isaiah, as something never to be forgotten by those who had heard it ; his love for such words as " Is not this the fast which I have chosen, to loose the bands of wickedness ; to undo the heavy burdens ; to let the oppressed go free and that ye break every yoke ? "   These words always remained in her mind as intimately associated with her memories of her father.

Happy in her childhood's home, she had the additional good fortune of a happy and early marriage.   George Butler, the eldest son of a Head Master of Harrow and subsequently Dean of Peterborough, was of an extremely modest and unpretentious character.   When questioned in later life, by the inevitable interviewer, about his youthful accomplishments, he replied, after a few moment's reflection, that he was considered to be " extremely good at shying stones."   But he could in fact, lay claim to great distinction as a Classical Scholar.   He was a distinguished Grecian and a favourite pupil of Dr. Wordsworth, afterwards Bishop of Lincoln.   Having migrated to Oxford in 1841, after only a year at Cambridge, George Butler was awarded the Hertford Scholarship, which I am told is Oxford's blue ribbon for Latin classical learning. He announced this with characteristic modesty to his friends. One of them, the Rev. Cowley Powles, describes the scene. He wrote, in after years : " I remember meeting him just after his success had been announced. I was coming back from a ride, and he stopped me and said : ' I have got the Hertford.' The announcement was made in his quietest voice and with no elation of manner though his countenance showed how much he was pleased." Two years later he was *facile princeps* for the Ireland Scholarship, but was considered by the examiners to be disqualified because he had not put down his name as a candidate within the specified number of days required. He was naturally disappointed but showed no trace of bitterness. He wrote to his father : " I may ' bear it as a man,' but I must also ' feel it as a man.' " The question had turned upon the point whether or not Sunday was to be counted as a day.

He, like his wife, was deeply and sincerely religious ; his intimates described him " as a child of Nature and a son of God." He had from boyhood onwards a remarkable native purity of mind and a loyal and reverent feeling towards women. The whole tendency of his mind and character inclined him to teaching as his profession. His father urged him, but for a long time in vain, to take orders ; he had a strong shrinking from this step and in one of his early letters to his future wife he write : " You know I don't like parsons . . . I shall never wear straight waistcoats, long coats and stiff collars . . . I have a longing to be of use and I know of no line in which I can be more useful than the educational, my whole life having been turned more or less in that direction. It is a blessed office that of a teacher." So a teacher he became. For four years he took pupils at Oxford and in 1848 he was appointed to a tutorship in the University of Durham. He wrote to his father while still at Durham : " I have no internal call and no inclination for the Church," and the influence of the little northern university appears to have been deterrent rather than otherwise to his taking orders. (*See* pp. 61-62, *Recollections of George Butler*.) He did, however, eventually become a clergyman. He weighed the matter a long time before coming to a decision ; and though there is no reason to suppose that he ever repented it, he remained to the end of his life essentially a layman and a scholar, rather than a cleric.

In her life of George Butler, his wife gives an amusing description of some of his boyish freaks ; for instance, he allowed his father, then Head Master of Harrow, to start for some ceremonial function in the School, involving full dress, with breeches and gaiters, having a gaiter on one leg but none on the other. On being remonstrated with for not calling his father's attention to this he excused himself on the ground that he did it " because it would so amuse the boys." (p. 7 *G.B.*) He was indeed, " full of humour but without mischief." As he grew up he became an expert in all sports and physical exercises, and was acknowledged at Oxford as one of the first classics of his time. He was also very good at modern languages and spoke French, Italian and German with ease and fluency. He was living in Oxford all through the fever of the Tractarian movement, and although he regarded several of its leaders with great respect, he never was the least attracted to it. He expressed his feelings on this subject in letters to his future wife in one of which he wrote : " I am sure Mary, who sat at the feet of Jesus, would have been puzzled by the reading over to her of the Athanasian Creed and the injunction to her to accept it all at the peril of the loss of her soul : but she understood what Jesus meant when He said ' One thing is needful ' and her knowledge of Him was enough to enable her to choose the better part." (Pp. 64-5, *Life of G.B.*)

George Butler and Josephine Grey were married at Dilston in January, 1852. They shortly afterwards settled at Oxford, which became their home for four years. Everything we know of them points to their having been attractive and popular members of a distinguished group of men and women. It was long before the days of married fellows and longer still before the foundation of women's colleges, so the society of which the Butlers formed part was in the main masculine and celibate.

Mr. Butler was something of an innovator in University matters ; he introduced new studies, such as geography. As I am writing this I observe in an evening paper that Bishop Creighton is quoted as having said that geography and history were the only two subjects really worth studying, for one involved all science and the other, all literature. So Mr. Butler was some 50 or 60 years in advance of his own times. " His geographical

Yrs very truly
George Butler

lectures," wrote his wife " were quite an innova-
tion, creating some amusement," as it had been
considered a subject only fit for young children
and incapable of the development and compre-
hensiveness which is now universally acknowledged.
He was one day engaged in drawing a rough map
of the Northern coast of Africa and part of Asia
Minor, when he was called on by a group of
Fellows and Tutors of colleges. The conversation
turned on Dean Stanley's letters describing his
visit to Egypt. One of the learned men present
had never heard of Damascus ! " Where is Cairo ? "
said another, and no one present could point even
approximately to the right place on the map or
be sure quite of the locality of Egypt !* And this,
notwithstanding the fame of Nelson's great victory,
which ought to have been known to every schoolboy
or girl.

No wonder that Mr. Butler's conviction was
strengthened that geography ought to be studied
in the University.

Mr. Butler was also instrumental in intro-
ducing the study of Art in Oxford ; he and his
wife were no mean artists, and to illustrate some
of his lectures they made copies of several of the
Turner Drawings in the Taylor Gallery. As an
artist Mr. Butler's drawings of the mountain
buttresses in the neighbourhood of Chamonix
had the honour of receiving high praise from
Ruskin, " Your outlines of these peaks, Mr.
Butler," he said, " are perfectly true. Very few

*The scene just described is referred to in a most decorous manner
in the Preface to a Public School Atlas which Mr. Butler edited for
Messrs. Longman in 1871.

people are able or care to represent them so cor-
rectly."

Mr. Butler also encouraged in Oxford the
serious study of modern languages, especially
Italian. He had formed a close friendship with
Aurelio Saffi, then living in Oxford exiled from
his native land. It will be remembered that Saffi,
together with Mazzini and Armellini, composed
the triumvirate which ruled Rome during the short-
lived republic of 1850, the story of which has been
so brilliantly told by Professor G. M. Trevelyan
in his Garibaldi trilogy. Mr. Butler's knowledge
of Italian was sufficiently wide and exact to enable
him to give valuable assistance to Dante Gabriel
Rossetti who was then engaged on his book *Dante
and his Circle*, and also on his translations of the
Vita Nuova and other early Italian writings.

It seems evident from the foregoing that the
Butlers were leading happy and useful lives in
Oxford, and that Mrs. Butler's subsequent develop-
ments are not to be attributed to any dissatisfaction
with her husband's position in the University or
to any personal disappointments or to doubtful
anticipations as to their future. Nevertheless,
there began to grow up in her mind a feeling
that all was not well with the pleasant and agree-
able society of which they formed a part.

How the feeling grew and strengthened will
be the subject of the next chapter.

CHAPTER III.

Oxford in the Fifties and Sixties. of the Last Century.

"There is a mystery that few understand—the power of vicarious suffering, and the grace of perpetual intercession—perhaps the noblest of all graces—the grace of a generous, prophet-like soul, which, in solitude and seclusion charges itself with the guilt of the community, mourning for the sins of the people."—Josephine Butler.

A TIME was approaching when Mrs. Butler could no longer feel herself at one with the brilliant and intellectually fascinating society in which she was placed. Not infrequently she sat silent ; listening, but not with sympathy, to the conversations she heard ; often she inwardly dissented with vehemence from the prevailing point of view which they revealed ; for the men about her spoke of things which she had already pondered deeply ; but she did not, in these early years, feel that she had knowledge or experience enough to enable her effectively to defend her own point of view. A novel had lately been written by Mrs. Gaskell in which the problem of the unmarried mother had been discussed with power and insight as well as with delicacy. This book was strongly condemned, however, by the Oxford of that day. Polite Oxford maintained that a pure woman should be absolutely ignorant that such evils existed in the world ; notwithstanding the fact that they bore with murderous cruelty on women. One young don seriously declared that he " would not allow his own mother to read such a book " as the one under discussion. The young pasha, it would seem, went far beyond either parental or marital authority ; sons were to dictate to mothers the books which it was suitable for them to read. By the law of reaction we have gone rather a long way on the other direction now. " Is it a play I could take Mama to ? " was a joke some twenty years ago ; but when a fallacy becomes a joke it has lost its sting ! At the time of which we are now writing silence was thought to be the one imperative duty on all these subjects. So far was the absolute embargo on raising moral questions as between the sexes carried, in general literature in the mid-nineteenth century, that Thackeray, when Editor of *The Cornhill*, declined a poem dealing with the subject by Elizabeth Barrett Browning. He admitted in his letter to her that she had written " pure doctrine and real modesty and pure ethics," but added that his readers would make an outcry and therefore he declined to publish the poem. " On one occasion," Mrs. Butler writes : " when I was distressed by a bitter case of wrong, inflicted on a very young girl, I ventured to speak to one of the wisest of men, so esteemed, in the University, in the hope that he could suggest some means, not of helping her, but of bringing to a sense of his crime the man who had wronged her. The sage, speaking kindly, however, sternly advocated silence and inaction. It would only do harm, he argued, if I opened up in any way such a question as this. It was dangerous to arouse a sleeping lion ; and I left him in amazement."

But for a long time Blake's terrible couplet rang in her ears :

" The harlot's curse from street to street
Shall weave old England's winding sheet."

Another horrible case of injustice came under her notice about this time . . . "A young mother was in Newgate for the murder of her infant, whose father, under cover of the death-like silence prescribed by Oxford philosophers—a silence which was in fact an endorsement of injustice—had perjured himself to her, had forsaken and forgotten her, and fallen back, with no accusing conscience upon his easy social life and possibly his academic honours." Mrs. Butler was nearly beside herself with rage at the injustice of it all. She wished to go and see its victim in prison and to speak to her of the God who saw the injustice and who cared for her. Fortunately, she told everything of what she was feeling to her husband. Then Mr. Butler did a beautiful thing. The 15th is often called the Gentleman's Psalm. It certainly presents a living portrait of George Butler. He did not say to his wife that it was hopeless to try to redress the wrong which had been done, that neither he nor she could recall the past or that what was done could not be undone ; instead of these rather useless truisms he said he would write to the Chaplain of Newgate and ask him to send the poor girl to them when her sentence had expired ; they wanted a servant and she might be able to fill the place. " She came to us," wrote Mrs. Butler, " I think she was the first of a world of unhappy women of a humble class whom he welcomed to his own home. She was not the last."

In these simple words Mrs. Butler, without knowing it, was writing her own life as well as that of the husband who shared all her aspirations and hopes of creating a better world for both men and women. For some years while they were still living in Oxford there was a little room in their house set apart for the reception of these poor waifs. Later, when living in Liverpool, the whole spare space in their much larger house was devoted to a similar purpose ; but as the number increased this plan became increasingly difficult and a House of Rest was hired in the city, as a haven for human wreckage.

Writing of her husband Mrs. Butler said : " That blessed gift of common sense, which he possessed in so large a degree, came to the rescue to restore for me the balance of a mind too heavily weighted with sad thoughts of life's perplexing problems. . . . And I said to myself 'And it is a man who speaks to me thus—an intelligent, a gifted man ; a learned man too, few more learned than he, and a man who ever speaks the truth from his heart.' So I was comforted and instructed."

During the American Civil War the Butlers were among the small band at Oxford who upheld the cause of the North. " Good practice," Mrs. Butler remarked, "in swimming against the stream": plenty of this practice lay ahead of her.

It was not the least of Mrs. Butler's trials that her husband was frequently and most unjustly blamed for her actions. He seconded her in every possible way, helping and supporting her ; but this did not shield either him or her from malicious attacks. At a later period of her life when she and her husband were living in Liverpool, he as the Principal of Liverpool College, she was virulently attacked for wanton cruelty to the poor girls whom she had done so much to befriend and rescue, and she felt bound, much as she disliked it, to speak of herself and of him who had been her right hand in all her work. It is almost incredible to us, who now know so much of her life and character, that she was actually accused, and by a man supposed to be a gentleman, of having treated these wretched girls with physical cruelty, spurning them with contumely and of doing her utmost to thrust them back into the mire from which they were emerging. She then felt bound to speak out and tell the truth. " I know," she said, " that when I speak though reluctantly, of what I myself have done, I am only recording what others have done with yet greater devotion. I have but one little spare room in my house. Into that little room I have received, with my husband's joyful assent, one after another of these my fallen sisters. We have given them, in the hour of trouble, sickness and death, the best that our house could afford. . . . In that little room I have nursed poor outcasts filled with disease and have loved them as if they have been my own sisters. Many have died in my arms. . . . I am ashamed to be driven to this self-defence, but I am still more ashamed that any English gentleman should have forced an English lady to put forth such a defence or record what we would rather for ever conceal, seeing that we have only done what it was our duty to do for the poor and sinful."*

When we speak now of Josephine Butler's Lifework we naturally think of her devotion to the outcasts of society and her determined opposition to the State regulation of vice. This is what James Stuart was thinking of when he wrote that the world was different and better because she had lived in it. But it must not be supposed that she looked on indifferent or hostile to the other branches of the Women's Movement. She was foremost among the early suffragists, and her signature is among those of the 1,499 who signed the Suffrage Petition to the House of Commons presented by John Stuart Mill in 1867, and she often referred publicly to the help her work would receive if women were enfranchised. She helped Henry Sidgwick, James Stuart, and Miss Clough to get what afterwards became Newnham College, started. She was one of those who in 1865 petitioned the Senate of the University of Cambridge to open their Local Examinations to girls ; she herself came up to Cambridge in support of the petition, and Miss A. J. Clough, the first Principal of Newnham College, wrote of her presence and influence on this occasion : " The charm Mrs. Butler put into all the details she gave, showing the desire of women for help in educating themselves, made the subject, which might have been considered tedious, both interesting and attractive and thus drew to our cause many friends." (p. 78, J.J.)

Her personal influence was, as always, very

*See Josephine Butler, a Life Sketch, by W. T. Stead, p. 20.

powerful. She describes some of the Cambridge Dons as deeply moved ; one in particular who, with tears in his eyes, said to her : " I fear we get selfish here and forget how much there is of work and sorrow in the world outside of us." Professor F. D. Maurice came to see her and talked very fully of the whole scheme in view, for helping forward the education of women. He said in taking leave of her : " If there is anything else which you and your friends think Cambridge could do to be of use, I trust you will suggest it ; it does *us* more good than it does to anyone else."

She became President of the North of England Council for the Higher Education of Women in 1867, and saw it rapidly developing in two directions ; towards the University Extension movement and the foundation of Newnham College. She never for a single moment believed that what was beneficial to women could be injurious to men, and would quote Professor Maurice's wise words : " Whenever . . . in any department of human activity restrictions tending to the advantage of one class and the injury of others have been removed, there, a Divine power has been at work counteracting not only these selfish calculations but often the apparently sagacious reasonings of their defenders."

Like others who have worked in some of the same fields she was never dismayed by the trite complacency with which she was often told that " Women's place is home," for not only was it easy to point out that this was the very place in which women were completely subordinate from the legal point of view, but that what was most wanted in the practical administrations of hospitals, workhouses, schools, orphanages, asylums and even prisons was the infusion of the home spirit and the setting free of feminine powers and influence for the humanising of these institutions.

The contrast between prisons, hospitals, workhouses, etc., as they exist to-day and as they existed in the time of Dickens is sufficient evidence of the practical value of women's share in the administration of the laws. Much of what Mrs. Butler foresaw fifty years ago has now actually taken place and is still taking place under our very eyes ; women are more and more taking their place as the mothers of the race in influencing not only the making of the laws but their practical administration.

Nothing was more remarkable in Mrs. Butler's personality than her spiritual power in influencing the minds and thoughts of others. We have seen already an instance of this in her husband. James Stuart was another whose mind was largely moulded by her ; and Frederick Myers whose poems " St. Paul " and " St. John the Baptist," are well known, revealed in his autobiographical sketch, called *Fragments of the Inner Life*, that Christianity came to him through the agency of Josephine Butler. " She introduced me to Christianity by an inner door, not to its encumbering forms and dogmas but to its heart of fire." His " St. Paul " was dedicated to J. E. B., with the inscription in Greek which declared that to her " he owed his very soul."

The late Canon Scott Holland also wrote of her in this sense and in deepest appreciation and gratitude " Few in this generation know the wonder and the beauty and the power put out over men of her own day by the personal heroism of Josephine Butler."

One young man with a well-known name, writes to her as his " Dearest friend " and ends his letter with the words " God be good to you, and bless your rest to you, for you will be serving Him then too, I know. Dearest mother, I love you much "

Another disciple she had in Dora Greenwell, who dedicated her work to J. E. B., with the inscription in Latin to the effect that " without thee nothing high my mind essays."*

Sometimes, when at Cambridge, she would see as many as 40 to 50 undergraduates, giving a short private talk to each. These conversations had an extraordinary and a lasting effect.

Sometimes even in quite recent times when I have been accidentally detained, waiting perhaps for a train that was taking me to my next meeting, I have ventured to ask my kind host or hostess what or who first attracted them to the subject we had been at work upon, be it women's suffrage or the League of Nations, and have received the reply : " Josephine Butler." People who were with her seem, in a very large number of cases, to have absorbed the spirit which animated Mary, the mother of Our Lord, when she said to the

*Recently, while this book is going through the press, I was at the annual meeting of a well-known women's society, when a lady came to speak to me whom I did not recognise. She told me she was Dame Katherine Furse, the daughter of the late John Addington Symonds. She added that lately, going through some of his M.S. papers, she came across one headed " Women who have most influenced me." The first name on this list was that of Josephine Butler.

servants at the marriage feast : " Whatsoever he saith unto you do it." Those people who have this power of the spirit have the making in them of great leaders and of these choice spirits, Josephine Butler was one.

At a time when neither Newnham nor Girton colleges existed, and the whole scheme for educating women in the older universities was in embryo, Miss Davies was only too apt to treat as enemies all those who did not accept her college as the only means of salvation.

Thus, for instance, she wrote to Mr. Henry Sidgwick in May, 1871 : *Your scheme is the serpent which is gnawing at our vitals*. (*See* p. 255, Life of Emily Davies, by Lady Stephen.) Mrs. Butler, on the other hand, after acting for many years as President of the North of England Council for promoting the higher education of women, was quite ready to make way for other schemes. She herself had favoured all along a more gradual approach to the citadel which she, like Miss Davies desired eventually to occupy. Mrs. Butler's letters describe an interview between herself and Miss Davies at a time when the latter was very much depressed about her college. " My objects," wrote Mrs. Butler, " are different from hers ; yet I can feel for her, and if it were not for the fear of a snub, I would write and comfort her, and tell her to hope in God about all schemes and to trust Him in spite of her own mistakes and failures. I wish well to her College and shall be grieved if it goes down ; only I would prefer beginning it humbly merely taking a house within reach of Cambridge and working up for the examinations given by the

Cambridge syndicate." All this is so characteristic of both the women that one almost seems on reading it to hear the sound of their voices.

Mrs. Butler's personal influence was so powerful that very few were able to resist the spell it cast upon them. She wrote in another letter of an interview with a pioneer woman who was an early leader in the political movement. Mrs. Butler describes her, perhaps unjustly, as bitter, hard and unimaginative," one in fact, who was detested by the ordinary man and woman. " One day," Mrs. Butler writes : " I had been talking affectionately to her and she, the great strong woman, suddenly fell on her knees at my feet with a passionate burst of weeping, said, ' O, if I could find love. May I love you ? You won't hate me as others do, you are just to women," I laid her head on my breast and soothed her. She sobbed like a child.

But she could be stern when the occasion required it, for instance, she soundly rated a well-known public man for his ignorance of economics and for the sentimental nonsense of his arguments on women's questions. Women according to him were to be worshipped and placed on pedestals, but were to be excluded from all paid employments, and were never to be admitted to the franchise but should be studiously kept in subjection. So much evil, as she had seen it exemplified in the " fallen woman," had arisen out of this economic subjection and exclusion from the better paid and more interesting employments, that it was no wonder that she wrote in reply to her antagonist, a letter of bitter reproach.

CHAPTER IV.

CHELTENHAM AND LIVERPOOL.

"It seems that some souls are elected more for the inner work than the outward ; but the honour conferred by such election is often slowly perceived and reluctantly accepted ; there is an anxious, sometimes a fretful urgency to be in the fore-front of the active work."
—JOSEPHINE BUTLER.

IN the autumn of 1856 Mrs. Butler had a serious breakdown in health. The winter floods which surrounded Oxford with water made it a deadly place to live in. After a very damp autumn in 1855, George Butler wrote in January, 1856 : " It rained all yesterday and to-day it is cold and damp. Indeed immediately after sunset the atmosphere of Oxford resembles that of a well, though that is scarcely so bad as the horrible smell of the meadows when the floods are retiring. Then one is conscious of a miasma which only a strong constitution can long resist." It appears, therefore, that " She is a fen of stagnant waters," was a line exactly applicable to the Oxford of that date, little as any one would think it so now.

His wife's failing health began to assume for Mr. Butler the phase of an ever present deep anxiety. The autumn of the same year fell damp and cold ; what was feared for Mrs. Butler was lung trouble ; and her husband resolved on taking her to London to consult Sir James Clarke. On hearing their story the physician said : " Poor thing, poor thing ¡ You must take her away from Oxford." They submitted and proposed returning at once to make the necessary preparations ; but even this was not allowed. " No," said the great doctor, " she must not return to the chilling influence of those floods, not for a single day." Therefore, in the autumn of 1856 they left Oxford never again to return to it as residents, and they had to face making another home under entirely different conditions. They then had a young family of three boys and one precious little girl, named Eva, a particularly bright and joyous child, the pet of the whole household.

The pecuniary circumstances of the Butlers at this period were difficult but not desperate. Mr. Butler wrote a good deal for the press and for periodicals. We hear, for instance, of his writing articles for *The Edinburgh Review*, and reviewing Tennyson's *Maud* for Fraser ; his other work of a similar kind doubtless brought grist to the mill. Mr. John Grey, Mrs. Butler's father, had had heavy losses through the failure of a bank and could not give the Butlers much assistance in the way of money. What he was to them in other ways requires no emphasis. Moreover, they had many and very devoted friends who were constantly on the watch for some way of serving them ; and in 1857 all anxiety as to ways and means was ended by the offer to Mr. Butler of the Vice-Principalship of Cheltenham College. They rejoiced in the change of climate and surroundings which Cheltenham afforded, and they were thankful for the provision of a large house in which Mr. Butler took pupils. He worked as a schoolmaster assiduously for the next twenty-five years, first at Cheltenham and then at the Liverpool College.

The Butlers, as ever, were taking a lively interest in the great events then unfolding themselves in other countries such as the American Civil War and the unification of Italy ; in the working out of this last, Mrs. Butler's favourite sister Harriet (Mme Meuricoffre), was privileged to take some personal share, as she had succeeded Jessie White Mario in the hospital care of the wounded Garibaldians and was personally acquainted with Garibaldi and with many of the leaders of his great movement.

But an overwhelming calamity lay ahead of Mrs. Butler and her husband, a calamity unforeseen, inexorable and cruel. In August, 1864, they had returned to Cheltenham after spending a few days with old friends in the Lake Country, when their only little girl was suddenly and tragically snatched from them. Running swiftly on an upper landing to meet her mother who was below, she suddenly lost her balance and fell over on the stone pavement at her mother's feet. She was not dead when the parents lifted her up, but she never spoke again, and at 10 o'clock that night the bright loving little spirit was with them no more. Mrs. Butler writing to a friend said : " These are weak words. May you never know the grief they hide rather than reveal. . . . It would be difficult to endure the shock of that agonising death . . . Little gentle spirit ! . . . Never can I lose that memory—the fall, the sudden cry, and then the silence ! It was pitiful to see her, helpless in her father's arms, her little drooping head resting on his shoulder, and her beautiful golden hair all stained with blood, falling over his arm. Would God that I had died for her ! " Mr. Stead says in his little book " Josephine Butler, a Life Sketch ": *Such was the call which first roused Josephine Butler to action.* Much as I appreciate the book I cannot agree with the words italicised ; Josephine Butler did not need such an awakening. She had taken action on behalf of the most despised and rejected of human beings long before this when she was an almost unknown woman in Oxford ; she had been foremost in her lifework of seeking and saving, and in offering friendship to the friendless, in helping them to understand not only that God loved them but that she, Josephine Butler, was their comrade and friend.

But of course, this heart-rending loss of her darling child left a lasting mark upon her whole nature. She did not allow herself to be selfish in her grief. What followed I must give in her her own words :

" This sorrow seemed to give in a measure a new direction to our lives and interests. There were some weeks of uncomforted anguish . . . Here there entered into the heart of our grief the intellectual difficulty, the moral plerpexity and dismay which are not the least terrifying of the phantoms which haunt the Valley of the Shadow of Death. That dark passage through which some toil only to emerge into a hopeless and final denial of the Divine Goodness . . . ; and others by the mercy of God, through a still deeper experience, into a yet firmer trust

in His unfailing love . . ."
" One day, going into his study, I found my husband alone and looking ill. His hands were cold, he had an unusual paleness in his face, and he seemed faint. I was alarmed. I kneeled beside him, and shaking myself out of my own stupor of grief, I spoke ' comfortably ' to him and forced myself to talk cheerfully, even joyfully, of the happiness of our child, of the unclouded brightness of her brief life on earth, and her escape from the trials and sorrows she might have met with had she lived. He responded readily to the offered comfort and the effort to strengthen him was helpful to myself. After this I often went to him in the evening after school hours, when sitting side by side, we spoke of our child in heaven, until our own loss seemed to become somewhat less bitter." (J. J., pp. 52-3.)

A dangerous illness overtook Mrs. Butler that same winter. As she advanced towards recovery it was arranged that she and her three boys, travelling by sea, should accompany Mme. Meuricoffre on her return to Italy. During this voyage Mrs. Butler was taken very seriously ill. Mme Meuricoffre wrote :

" My heart was praying desperately to God that He would make a way of escape, that He would work a miracle for us. *And He did*. The three boys went away and we all prayed to God to save her. After a time I felt a hand on my shoulder. It was the Captain. He said : ' I saw the other mail vessel coming north. I have signalled her. If she sees us you shall

go on board and return to Leghorn. Make
haste.' I drew a long breath, and said, ' Thank
God, I think we are saved.' I felt the horror
melting away in a measure and hope springing
up. We rolled her up and I went for the
children and found a kind young Sicilian officer
comforting them. I thanked him. He said in
Italian something about the love of Christ, so
kindly. I said very little about her. But
people must have been impressed by her look
and thought her dying to take such extreme
measures as to stop two Government steamers
on the high seas."

Mrs. Butler and her three sons took passage
again in calmer weather and spent several months
in the Meuricoffre household in Italy.

The Butlers had always taken a very international view of public affairs. Since their marriage
they had had almost annual holidays in various
parts of Europe and they were not content with
the ordinary tourist round of picture galleries and
fine sights. They had sought and found true
friendship among leading citizens of the various
countries they had visited. This was of great
advantage to her and the work she afterwards so
devotedly undertook, and we find from the records
of the letters and journals that she had a remarkable
group of friends in many of the leading nations
of Europe and America, among whom I may
mention Victor Hugo, Yves Guyot, Pére Hyacinthe,
Mazzini, Garibaldi, Emile de Laveleye of
Belgium, and W. Lloyd Garrison of the U.S.A.

When the time came for her to be the leader
of a great international movement against the

State Regulation of Vice she was already provided with a band of invaluable friends and helpers in various countries. Her husband's removal from Cheltenham to the Principalship of the Liverpool College in 1865-6 was also a help in the same direction. For Liverpool, by its size and importance as the second largest port in Great Britain or in the world, had in many senses an international character, and the college was a faithful representative of the city in this respect. Among its eight to nine hundred pupils there were Greeks, Armenians, Jews, Negroes, Americans, French, Germans and Spaniards, and two sons of half-civilised African chiefs. These, of course, represented a great variety of religious faiths.

Mrs. Butler was, therefore, more than usually well equipped for undertaking the international work which soon after this awaited her. But her first task was to grapple with the evil of the social slavery of state regulated vice in its national aspects.

Josephine Butler

CHAPTER V.

THE BEGINNING IN ENGLAND OF THE CAMPAIGN
AGAINST THE CONTAGIOUS DISEASES
ACTS.

*"There is no evil in the world so great that God
cannot raise up to meet it, a corresponding beauty and
glory which will blaze it out of countenance."—*
J. E. B. (Address in Edinburgh, 1871.)

BEFORE describing the struggle for the
Abolition of the C. D. Acts which Mrs.
Butler so ably led and with which her
name will always be associated, it will be
well to give a short survey of the position in
our own country on this question before 1869.

Prostitution is a very ancient institution. It
has its roots in the old belief that " the irregular
indulgence of a natural impulse "* is right for men
and wrong for women. Yet a man cannot have
this " irregular indulgence " unless he can find a
woman to be his partner. If the majority of women
are to be " regular," while the majority of men
are " irregular," it follows that there must be a
small body of women to whom large numbers of
men can resort, and that this condition of things
must inevitably lead to social disorder and disease.
Men have, from time to time, attempted to deal
with this disorder and disease by regulation or

* This phrase is quoted from the Report of the Royal Commission
of 1870 to enquire into the working and administration of the Contagious
Diseases Bills of 1864, 1868, and 1869.

The Life and Work of

suppression. Both methods have been aimed solely
at the women who were alleged to be prostitutes,
and no attempt was made to deal with the vastly
greater body of men who consorted with them, and
who were, if only by reason of their greater numbers
a far graver source of danger to the general community. It is impossible to read the history of
prostitution without a deep feeling of indignation
at the stupidities and injustices perpetrated against
unfortunate and sometimes innocent women in the
name of health, public order and even religion.

In England except for a short period, when the
brothels adjoining the episcopal palace of the
Bishop of Winchester were given a royal licence,*
no attempt was made to licence or regulate prostitution until 1864, though there had been various
repressive statutes at different times. Perhaps as
some set off to this disgrace to Winchester, readers
may like to call to mind the well-known story of
Thomas Ken in 1685, who when resident in
Winchester and Chaplain to King Charles II,
sturdily refused the Royal demand that he should
provide a lodging for Nell Gwyn on the occasion
of a visit of the Court to the city. The sequel
to this story is interesting : for a year later, the
Bishopric of Bath and Wells, being vacant, the
question who should fill it was raised in the Privy
Council, when Charles exclaimed " Where is the
good little man who refused a lodging to poor

* Henry II assented to an Act " for licensing the stews of South-
wark " (Act 8. Henry II. 1161). These houses belonged to the Bishop
of Winchester of whom they were farmed by capitalists. They were
sacked by Watt Tylor as a protest against the licentiousness of the
rulers and clergy. Henry II's Act was confirmed in 1345, in 1391, and
1393, modified in 1506 and in 1545 abolished together with the houses.
(Quoted from " A State Iniquity," by Benjamin Scott, F.R.A.S.)

40

Nell ? " and insisted that Ken should have the vacant see. One sometimes forgets that Charles II was the grandson of Henry of Navarre, and great grandson of Jeanne D'Albret.

The cause of the introduction of an Act in 1868 to regulate prostitution was the alarm, quite sincerely felt, at the increase in disease, not only among the men of the army and navy, but also among the civil population, especially where it was congregating in ever increasing numbers in industrial centres. The authorities had reason for alarm : but the alarm was exploited by those who wished to set up in this country a system of Regulation of Prostitution modelled on that introduced into France in 1802 by Napoleon I, and had already been copied by several other European countries. About 1860 this system was regarded almost without exception by doctors and police administrators as the only method of dealing effectively with prostitution, although even at that time evidence was already accumulating (as Mrs. Butler pointed out in a pamphlet issued in 1870*), that it was " ineffectual to stamp out disease."

Under the French system registered women, *i.e.*, " prostitutes," were set apart in certain houses, " tolerated " or licensed by the police or municipal authorities, where the inmates could be medically examined at stated intervals and kept under the control of specially appointed police and surgeons. This was the system, with certain modifications, which was introduced into this country in 1866 : with this difference that, whereas, in France, it was purely a police measure, in England it was

* "An Appeal to the People of England." J. Butler, 1870.

inaugurated by Act of Parliament.* While this gave an official encouragement to prostitution that even a French administration had never dared to insist upon, it laid the system much more open to effective attack. The first Contagious Diseases Prevention Act (Women) was passed in 1864, other Acts were passed in 1866, and 1869. They applied at first only to fourteen military and naval stations, but it was intended by degrees to extend their operation throughout the entire country.

The main features of the Acts were :
(1) Registration and police supervision of prostitutes.
(2) Their periodical medical examination for the detection of venereal disease.
(3) Their compulsory detention in special hospitals if diseased.

Mrs. Butler always maintained that the C. D. Acts were a violation of English Law. Her book " The Constitution Violated," published in 1870, substantiates the charge. She takes the provisions of Magna Charta and Habeas Corpus, and, by comparing them with the provisions of the Contagious Diseases Acts, shows that women (and not only known prostitutes, but all women " suspected of being prostitutes ") were deprived of the safeguards and personal security hitherto established by law ; that they were liable to punishment for an offence that was not an offence in law ; and that they were liable, on the mere suspicion of a policeman, to arrest and a forced medical examination. If they resisted this examination they were imprisoned with hard labour. Mrs. Butler's book cannot be effectively quoted, it should be read by

* In England women were not obliged to live in special houses.

all those who would understand what this infamous system meant. They will also get a vivid picture of Mrs. Butler herself; the passion for justice which was the mainspring of her life, expresses itself in the vivid prose of her book.

The first C. D. Act had been passed through Parliament in 1864 mainly as the result of the findings of a Royal Commission, appointed in 1859, to inquire into " the sanitary state of the Army in India." Another Committee had been appointed in 1862 to inquire into " the state of disease in the Army and Navy and to report on the working of the Regulation of prostitution in foreign parts," but the report of this Committee, though received, was not published : the evidence was unfavourable to Regulation and the Committee reported against its publication. By this time the English Government had determined to introduce some system of Regulation and they proceeded, as we have already shown, to pass the first C. D. Act through Parliament in 1864, with as little publicity as possible. The general public was probably ignorant of the Act ; it was certainly indifferent. But there had already been important opposition. The *Daily News* had published, on the 4th, 10th, and 23rd September, 1862, four leading articles and a letter by Miss Harriet Martineau, proving the futility of regulation and pointing out other, and better methods of dealing with disease. Meanwhile the Government had appointed a Medical Committee which reported in 1866 in favour of the periodical compulsory examination of women ; and a Select Committee of the House of Commons reported in favour of a further Contagious Diseases

Bill. This Bill became law in 1866 and replaced the 1864 Act which had expired. In the debate in the House of Commons on the principle of the Acts, the only dissenting voices recorded were two—those of the Rt. Hon. J. W. Henley, Conservative member for Oxfordshire, and Mr. A. S. Ayrton, Radical member for the Tower Hamlets. These two members presented a complete contrast in almost every respect. Mr. Henley was a representative of the best type of the scholarly English country gentleman, while Mr. Ayrton, was a Radical of undoubted courage but also of undoubted unpopularity. In 1868 a further amendment of the 1866 Act received the Royal Assent. Then, at last, opposition to the Acts began to take form. The Rev. Dr. Hoopell wrote a letter to the Press exposing and denouncing the Acts ; and Mr. Daniel Cooper, the Secretary of the London Rescue Society (realising after an interview with Mr. Berkeley Hill the leader of the Pro-Act party , their unjust and unscientific nature) became an active opponent. He was joined by Mr. Sheldon Amos and in 1869 by Dr. Bell Taylor, and Dr. Worth of Nottingham. Miss Wolstenholme (afterwards Mrs. Elmy), Dr. Elizabeth Blackwell and Miss Martineau (who, as recorded above, had made her first protest as early as 1862), protested against the Acts. A memorandum was drawn up by Mr. Cooper and sent to every Member of Parliament, to the principal clergy of the Church of England, and to the leading Nonconformist ministers. But there was little response to this appeal, and the C. D. Act of 1869 was placed on the Statute Book. The protesters were in despair. They

were a small body without political influence in
the country, and they were regarded as sentimental
faddists. In their despair they turned to Mrs.
Butler, and at Dr. Bell Taylor's request Miss
Wolstenholme telegraphed to her. This part of
the story is best told in Mrs. Butler's own words :

> " The names of Dr. Charles Bell Taylor and
> Dr. Worth of Nottingham, must be gratefully
> remembered, for it was to those gentlemen
> that we, the women of England, owed our
> first clear information of the nature and the
> passing of the Act of 1869. I had been on the
> Continent with my family in that year, and
> had been learning much there concerning the
> disastrous effects of this system. On the journey
> home, I found a telegram awaiting me at
> Dover, begging an interview, and this was
> followed by a somewhat mysterious appeal
> from these alert friends at Nottingham to
> ' haste to the rescue.' In a few days the whole
> state of the case was put before me and a small
> group of friends. No organised action, however,
> was taken by us until the close of December
> of that year. In fact, there was much preparation
> of heart, nerve and mind necessary for such
> a task as was now opening out before us. It
> was not a thing to be taken up hastily."*

It is perhaps almost impossible for us to realise
to-day how much courage and conviction was
needed for a woman to challenge public opinion
on this subject. But Mrs. Butler had counted
the cost. She has told the story in her books
" Personal Reminiscences of a Great Crusade,"

* " Personal Reminiscences of a Great Crusade."

and her " Memoir of George Butler," in her own
graphic way, and it should be read there. She
knew, when she answered the call, what it would
mean for herself and those she loved. She was
intensely unhappy at the thought of the work
which lay before her ; especially as she knew she
would not suffer alone, but that her husband would
share with her the obloquy she would bring down
upon herself.

" My heart," she wrote,* " was shaken by the
foreshadowing of what I knew he would suffer.
I went to him one evening when he was alone
. . . I recollect the painful thoughts that pursued
me during that passage from my room to his
study. I hesitated and leaned my cheek against
his closed door ; and as I leaned I prayed. Then I
went in and gave him something I had written
and left him. I did not see him again until
the next day. He looked pale and troubled, and
for some days was silent. But by and by we
spoke together freely and we agreed that we
must move in the matter and that an appeal
must be made to the people . . . I spoke to my
husband then of all that had passed in my
mind, and said : ' I feel as if I must go out
into the streets and cry aloud, or my heart
will break.' And that good and noble man,
foreseeing what it meant for me and himself,
spoke not one word to suggest difficulty or
danger or impropriety in any action which I
might be called to take. He did not pause to
ask : ' What will the world say ? ' or ' Is this
suitable work for a woman ? ' He had pondered

Memoir of George Butler. Chap. IX.

the matter, and looking straight, as was his wont, he saw only a great wrong, and a deep desire to redress that wrong, a duty to be fulfilled in fidelity to that impulse, and in the cause of the victims of the wrong ; and above all, he saw God, who is of ' purer eyes than to behold iniquity,' and whose call (whatever it be) it is man's highest honour to obey ; and his whole attitude in response to my words cited above, expressed, ' Go ! and God be with you.' "

Once she had taken the first difficult step, her courage rose to meet the storm, and she inspired the gallant band of men and women who gathered round her with an equal courage and devotion. " Mrs. Butler was," says Dr. Bell Taylor, " the head and front of the movement throughout ; her beauty, her grace, her eloquence and indomitable courage won adherents on every side and secured the victory for us at last."

The first Association formed to oppose the Acts was founded on October 5th, 1869, at Bristol, following the meeting of the Social Science Congress where the Acts had been discussed, and, on a motion by Dr. Bell Taylor, a resolution of protest had been carried by a large majority. This Association was the " National Association for the Repeal of the Contagious Diseases Acts." Almost simultaneously the Ladies' National Association for the same purpose was formed and the two Societies worked together in the closest harmony until the victory was won in 1886.

Concerning the Ladies' National Association, Mr. Daniel Cooper wrote to Mrs. Butler : " I tell you candidly I felt an almost utter despair in seeing that after putting forth our pamphlet, and writing thousands of letters, imploring our legislators, clergy, principal public men and philanthropists to look into the question, such a stoical indifference remained. We felt, on hearing of your Association, that Providence had well chosen the means for the defeat of these wicked Acts. The Ladies of England will save the country from this fearful curse ; for I fully believe that through them it has even now had its death blow. The men who charge ladies foremost in the struggle with indelicacy are not worthy of the name of men. As to our Members of Parliament, pray do not excuse their ignorance ; do not try to palliate their error by saying the Act was passed at the fag end of the session. The papers placed in their hands by ourselves, the letters of warning we addressed to them, leave them no excuse. Knowing, as none but ourselves can know, what was done to arouse them, I cannot but conclude that, with a few honourable exceptions our Members of Parliament cared nothing about the matter until public opinion forced them to look into it. But for the Ladies' National Association we should have had no discussion, and the Acts would by this date have probably been extended throughout the country. I say this solemnly, and from an intimate knowledge of all the plans of the Association formed to extend these Acts."

The Ladies' National Association immediately began to collect signatures for their manifesto against the Acts and on December 31st, 1869, it was published in the *Daily News*. It is quoted here in full, for it is a historic document and the names of those who dared to sign it ought never to be forgotten by Englishwomen.

" We, the undersigned, enter our solemn Protest against these Acts—

" 1st.—Because, involving as they do, such a momentous change in the legal safeguards hitherto enjoyed by women in common with men, they have been passed, not only without the knowledge of the country, but unknown to Parliament itself ; and we hold that neither the Representatives of the People, nor the Press, fulfil the duties which are expected of them, when they allow such legislation to take place without the fullest discussion.

" 2nd.—Because, so far as women are concerned they remove every guarantee of personal security which the law has established and held sacred, and put their reputation, their freedom, and their persons absolutely in the power of the police.

" 3rd.—Because the law is bound, in any country professing to give civil liberty to its subjects, to define clearly an offence which it punishes.

" 4th.—Because it is unjust to punish the sex who are the victims of a vice, and leave unpunished the sex who are the main cause, both of the vice and its dreaded consequences ; and we consider that liability to arrest, forced surgical examination, and (where this is resisted) imprisonment with hard labour, to which these Acts subject women, are punishments of the most degrading kind.

" 5th.—Because, by such a system, the path of evil is made more easy to our sons, and to the whole of the youth of England ; inasmuch as a moral restraint is withdrawn the moment the State recognises, and provides convenience for, the practice of a vice which it thereby declares to be necessary and venial.

" 6th.—Because these measures are cruel to the women who come under their action—violating the feelings of those whose sense of shame is not wholly lost and further brutalising even the most abandoned.

"7th.—Because the disease which these Acts seek to remove has never been removed by any such legislation. The advocates of the system have utterly failed to show, by statistics or otherwise, that these regulations have in any case, after several years' trial, and when applied to one sex only, diminished disease, reclaimed the fallen, or improved the general morality of the country. We have, on the contrary, the strongest evidence to show that in Paris and other continental cities where women have long been outraged by this forced inspection, the public health and morals are worse than at home.

" 8th.—Because the conditions of this disease, in the first instance, are moral, not physical. The moral evil through which the disease makes its way separates the case entirely from that of the plague, or other scourges, which have been placed under police control or sanitary care. We hold that we are bound, before rushing into the experiment of legalising a revolting vice, to try to deal with the *causes* of the evil, and we dare to believe that with wiser teaching and more capable legislation, those causes would not be beyond control."*

The manifesto roused the supporters of the Acts. It was greeted with a storm of anger and abuse. But it was a trumpet call to the opponents of the Acts and on every side men and women hastened to answer it.

" They rise before me now," wrote Mrs. Butler,† " those groups of faces of dear friends and companions in labour, of all classes and conditions, and of different lands and races. Many have passed away; but their memory lives in the hearts of those with whom they were associated for a time in work and prayer and hope.

" First among the many groups comes that of the earliest and most active leaders in the Ladies' National Association . . . I refer especially to the sisters Priestman and Margaret Tanner, with Miss Estlin and others closely associated with them, who have been to me, personally, through this long struggle, from the first years till now, a kind of body-guard, a *corps d'élite* on whose prompt aid, singleness of purpose, prudence and unwearying industry, I could and can rely at all times, and the knowledge of whose existence and loyalty alone, even when parted from them for long periods, is a continued source of comfort and strength. The utter absence in them of any desire for recognition, of any vestige of egotism in any

---

* Personal Reminiscences of a Great Crusade.
† Personal Reminiscences.   Chap. VI.

form, is worthy of remark. In the purity of their motives they shine out ' clear as crystal.' " The mere mention of their names, and those of a host of others, is but a cold and poor tribute. Nevertheless, I cannot pass on without a brief allusion to others. Mrs. Kenway, of Birmingham, was another of my strongest friends ; her house was always my home in passing through and working in that busy centre, a home in which I was always lovingly received by herself, her husband, and all her family. I must mention her sister also, Mrs. Henry Richardson, of York. Other names which crowd upon me are those of Mrs. Edward Walker, of Leeds, Mr. and Mrs. Clark, of Newcastle, Mr. and Mrs. Spence Watson, and the Richardson family of the same town ; of Mrs. Pease Nichol, Miss Wigham, and Mrs. Bright McLaren, of Edinburgh ; of Mrs. Lucas, Mrs. Maclaren and other ladies of Glasgow, and Miss Isabella Tod, of Belfast, one of the ablest, and certainly the most eloquent of our women workers of those times. Miss Lucy Wilson, whose loss to our cause, through death, some years ago was a serious one, might be numbered as one of the legal helpers of our cause. She had a remarkably keen intelligence, and extraordinary capacity for sifting evidence, unravelling tortuous argument, and dividing the true from the false. She was often employed by our Parliamentary friends to examine and pronounce upon doubtful proposals, emanating from the Government or elsewhere. Her verdict was generally found to be just. Her character

and feelings as a woman, at the same time, were
true and tender.*

" There are many more names—revered and
honourable—which I might bring in, but as I do
not know how to enumerate them, I am forced,
like the Apostle who gives us the record of the
heroes of faith, to sum up with the words :
'And what shall I say more ?   For time would
fail me to tell ' of this and that standard-
bearer of righteousness.   Their record is in
heaven ; they do not need my poor homage ;
they never coveted earthly praise."—*Personal
Reminiscences of a Great Crusade.*

In the early days of 1870 the campaign was
definitely launched.   Mrs. Butler addressed her
first meeting at the Friends' Meeting House,
Leeds, and then went to Crewe where she addressed
her first meeting of men only.   They were mainly
railway workers.   When she had finished, a small
group of leaders among these men came forward
and bade her thrice welcome in the name of all
there.   They said :   " We understand you perfectly.   We, in this group, have served an appren-
ticeship in Paris and we have seen and know for
ourselves the truth of what you say.   We have said
to each other that it would be the death knell of
the moral life of England if she were to copy France
in this matter."

The first number of " The Shield " was
published on March 7th, 1870.   From that time to

---

* I cannot refrain from adding to this list the names of Mr. Percy
Bunting and his wife, and of Mrs. Sheldon Amos, their sister-in-law ;
they were most staunch, and Mr. Bunting's position as Editor of the
Contemporary Review gave him a pulpit, as it were, from which he
could set forth the principles of the Repealers.—M. G. F.

the present day (with a break of eleven years from
1886 to 1897) it has in weekly, monthly, or quarterly
form continued its propaganda for the principles
advocated by Mrs. Butler. Meetings were held,
literature published, statistics and information
collected, memorials and petitions were signed;
and slowly, but none the less surely, a tide of
indignation began to rise against the Acts.

It may be well to mention here that it was
frequently stated, both publicly and privately
at the time when the discussion upon the policy
of the Acts was at its hottest, that it was but just
that the legislation should have been directed
mainly against women, because it was women who
acted as temptresses, and that men might therefore
be regarded as comparatively innocent victims.
Of course there may have been instances in which
this was the case, but on the other hand there were
innumerable instances in which the " solicitation "
was by men addressed by them to perfectly modest
and well behaved women. Two instances of this
came to my own knowledge in 1870. The first
was that of a young gentlewoman then engaged
on literary work in the office of " The Shield,"
as sub-editor. She was walking under an umbrella
on a rainy November evening, when she was
startled by the sudden appearance of a man's
head under her umbrella uttering the words :
" May I have the pleasure of escorting you home ? "
She, with quick wit, retorted : " I will escort
you to a policeman." The head was instantaneously
and rapidly withdrawn and she saw no more of
its owner than two legs rapidly vanishing into the
fog. The other case of male solicitation which

came to my knowledge about the same time happened in broad daylight in a crowded thorough-fare. A young woman, quietly and simply dressed, was passing along the street in London between the Bank and the Royal Exchange at about 12 noon, a man from behind her suddenly put his head over her shoulder and said in a low voice, but slowly and distinctly : " I will give you £2 if you will come with me." She said not one word, but hailed a hansom cab which was passing, and slipped away without further misadventure, to her own home. These two incidents which came to my knowledge within a short time left no doubt in my mind that solicitation in a bad sense was not confined to one sex, and that hundreds of similar impertinences were being addressed by scoundrels to poverty-stricken working girls every day.

CHAPTER VI.

THE COLCHESTER ELECTION, 1870.

BEFORE relating further the history of the Campaign, it will be advisable to set down briefly the motives and arguments of the opposing parties. The promoters of the Contagious Diseases Acts believed that it was necessary to provide for the " irregular indulgence of a natural impulse " in men. Given that necessity they argued that the logical method of dealing with it was to regulate and control the means of satisfying it. They recognised that the indulgence caused disease and disorder ; their remedy was to set up a severe medical and police control of prostitutes. Many of them believed quite sincerely that no moral considerations must be allowed to stand in the way of health measures that would be—in their view—adequate and necessary.* Others were convinced that the C. D. Acts had both moral and religious sanction, because they were supposed to have a reformative and restraining influence on the women who came under their operation. These points of view were expressed by the *Saturday Review* (1874) as the following extract shows :

* The following statistics are a sufficient comment on this view. The figures for venereal disease in the Home Army in 1883 *after eighteen years of regulation* were 260 per 1,000 or almost exactly the same as they had been in 1865. In 1924 *after thirty-eight years of non-regulation* the figures were 25˙2 per 1,000. (*See* Report on the Health of the Army for the Year 1924. Vol. LX. 1926.)

" Governments with real responsibility upon them must be content to trust that what is required for the health of people is the most in harmony with Christianity."

To these arguments the Repealers replied that there was no proof that prostitution was necessary, or that men were necessarily, and by nature, incapable of chastity.

" This admission," said Miss Harriet Martineau, " of the necessity of vice is the point on which the whole argument turns and on which irretrievable consequences depend. Once admitted the necessity of a long series of fearful evils follows as of course. There can be no resistance to seduction, procuration, disease and regulation, when once the original necessity is granted. Further, the admission involves civil as well as military society, and starts them together on the road which leads down to what moralists of all ages and nations have called the lowest hell."

Moreover, the Repealers argued that in placing a body of women—already outcast—so completely in the hands of a special police, created for that purpose, the promoters of the C. D. Acts were building up a system of tyranny and corruption in public administration, which must be inimical to public order and public morality alike. On the medical side they pointed out that no scheme, however severe, or well administered, could prevent clandestine prostitution ; or insure that even those women who could be placed on the register, would not be infected by some client between the periodical examinations they were required to undergo.

Josephine Butler's deepest reason for her attack

on the Acts was that they violated human liberty
and were founded on injustice. " It was," she
says, " as a citizen of a free country first, and as a
woman secondly, that I felt impelled to come
forward in defence of right." She was prepared
to take her stand against Regulation *even if it
could have been proved effective from the administrative and medical standpoint, because it was an attack
upon human liberty.* Again and again throughout
her writings and speeches that idea is insisted on,
it is indeed the keynote of her philosophy. She
wrote :

" It is perhaps in England alone that the depriva-
tion of civil rights, which such legislation
involves for the class it immediately affects,
should have also necessarily included the whole
of womanhood obviously and confessedly in
the class of aggrieved persons. For the constitution of this country is such, that the violation
of the civil rights of any class is felt necessarily
as a blow to the whole community. It so happened in England such a system could not be
carried out without transgressing, confessedly
and openly, the time honoured constitutional
barriers which have been the strength and
safety of our land. English men, and above all,
English women, could not see these violated
and broken down in any class, even the lowest,
without foreseeing all that must follow, and
without recognising in an injustice done to the
meanest citizen, an injury done to themselves."

Mrs. Butler was the leader and inspirer of the
opposition to the Acts. Some idea of her activity
may be gained from the fact that between June,

1869, and June 1870, she had addressed 99 public meetings and four conferences and had travelled for that purpose over 3,700 miles. The first Repeal Bill was introduced into the House of Commons the same year, and the Repealers began to take part in bye-elections.

A political change had, however, recently taken place which favourably affected the whole situation from Mrs. Butler's point of view. In 1868 Disraeli had carried his Reform Bill, which greatly extended the franchise and virtually established household suffrage in the boroughs throughout Great Britain (for men only, of course, at this date). This created an electorate in which the working class, who knew most and cared most about the operation of the Contagious Diseases Acts, were in a considerable majority. It is not clear that the party of Abolition were at the outset aware of the importance of this change ; but it was soon revealed to them by actual experience. At a bye-election at Newark in 1870, Sir Henry Storks, a notorious supporter of the regulation system, retired rather than face the opposition of the Abolitionists. In October of that year, a vacancy occurred at Colchester, and Sir Henry Storks again became the Government candidate ; this time he did not retire, and of course the Repealers opposed him as vigorously as before. A Liberal Government was in power, and the Repealers had to face considerable indignation from the Liberal Party (to which many of them belonged) for their opposition to the Government candidate. (The same situation arose years later over the Women's Suffrage Controversy when many keen Liberals had to oppose their own party candidates for the sake of a principle that was stronger than party.) Sir Henry Storks had the support, not only of the Government and his own party but of other elements in the constituency who were interested in the persistence of the Regulation system, and these elements bent all their efforts towards making it impossible for the Repealers even to stay in Colchester. If it had not been for the serene courage and self-possession of Mrs. Marriage, a well-known Quaker of the district, it would have been almost impossible for Mrs. Butler, Mr. Stuart, and Dr. Baxter Langley (who had allowed himself to be nominated as the Repeal candidate), to organise any campaign there.

There was scarcely ever an election more fiercely contested. It is a thrilling story to read, even now nearly sixty years later. Mrs. Butler and her supporters went about in peril of their lives and had to be concealed in secret hiding places such as hay lofts and underground cellars. It was a grim business but we cannot help hoping that she had relief now and then in some of its lighter interludes ; as, when being pursued by a howling mob, a kind grocer rescued her and smuggled her, first into his back shop, and then, for additional safety, into a fortress which he had created in his cellar where she was safely ensconced behind his battlements of soap and candles.

As this bye-election was an important landmark in the struggle for repeal the following account of it, taken from "A State Iniquity,"* is given at some length.

*A State Iniquity. By Benjamin Scott, City Chamberlain (1814-1892).

" The Repealers' Campaign was commenced by the holding of earnest prayer meetings, whereat they gained strength and courage. Then they went into the streets. They distributed thousands of handbills containing Sir Henry Storks' views on prostitution, and a statement made by him to the House of Commons Committee that ' not only prostitutes but also soldiers' wives ought to be examined.' The blood of the Liberal partisans was up. They attacked the hotel in which Mrs. Butler and her friends were staying, and when Dr. Baxter Langley began to hold public meetings they went mad and created a riot. Dr. Langley tried to hold a meeting in the theatre, but he and Professor Stuart were scarcely able to announce their principles before they were driven from the platform and chased to their hotel, which they reached, Langley covered with flour and dirt from head to foot, his clothes torn, his face bleeding, and Stuart wounded in the arm by a heavy blow which some ruffian had inflicted with a chair. The followers of Storks may have justified this playfulness as one of the amenities of political warfare but there was no sort of justification for the next thing they did. They posted on the walls an exact description of Mrs. Butler's dress in order that she might be recognised and mobbed. Every day she had to alter her dress, and her friends never addressed her by name in the street lest some listener should rally the ever-ready mob to attack her. One after another, hotel and lodging-house keepers dismissed her from their houses. On one occasion, after repeated flights from different houses, a room was taken for her in a Tory Hotel, under the name of Grey. There she had gone to bed and was falling asleep when she heard a knock at the door of her room, followed by the shout of the proprietor : ' Madam, I am sorry to find you are Mrs. Butler ; please get up and dress at once and leave the house. The mob are round the house breaking the windows. They threaten to set fire to it if you don't leave at once. They have found out you are here. Never mind your luggage, leave it here ; dress quickly, and I will show you out at the back door.' Then he harangued the mob whilst Mrs. Butler was dressing, and led by one of the servant girls ran along a little back street as fast as they could go, until she found shelter in the humble house of a kind-hearted woman. The next morning it was seen that the doors of the hotel had been shattered by stones.

" The women's prayer meetings were maintained throughout the contest, but the ruffian supporters of Storks unrestrained if not egged on to their ruffianism by their local leaders, tried to prevent them. They gathered about the door of the hall where the meetings were held, and brandished their fists in the faces of the women as they entered, greeting and following them with oaths and curses, and their ceaseless yells outside drowned the praying voices within the hall, which they loudly threatened to burn down. The violence of passion was not limited to the street mob.

A Wesleyan minister in the town wrote a letter against Storks, and for thus daring to express a righteous opinion not held by his infuriated flock, these pious folk drove him from his church and the town."

But in spite of this violence, perhaps even because of it, a vast amount of sympathy and encouragement for the Repealers and their cause was manifested by the people of Colchester. Mrs. Butler quotes the following amusing incident.

" I met an immense workman, a stalwart man trudging along to his home after work hours. By his side trotted his wife, a fragile woman, but with a fierce determination on her small thin face. At that moment she was shaking her little fist in her husband's face, and I heard her say : ' Now you know all about it ; if you vote for that man Storks, Tom, I'll kill you.' Tom seemed to think that there was some danger of her threat being put into execution. This incident did not represent exactly the kind of influence which we had entreated the working women to use with their husbands who had votes, but I confess it cheered me not a little."

It was not considered safe for Mrs. Butler to remain in the town on the day of the declaration of the poll. She and her friends had made a secret code among themselves. Sir Henry Storks, owing to his name, was referred to as " the bird," and the news of his overwhelming defeat at the poll was communicated to her in the words of the telegram : " bird shot dead." Storks had been defeated by more than 500 votes. The numbers were: Colonel Learmonth (C) 1364, Sir Henry Storks (L) 853.

Sir Henry Stork's defeat was a great blow to the Government, who began to realise that the opposition to the C. D. Acts was something more than an unimportant agitation by a small group of fanatics. They decided to shelter themselves and gain time by setting up a Royal Commission to report on the working and administration of the Acts. The Commission was appointed on November 23rd, 1870, and held its first session on December 14th. The Repealers, who considered that they had the country behind them in their demand for complete repeal of the Acts, did not approve of the appointment of this Commission, for they saw in it a shrewd move by the Government to paralyse the agitation against the Acts and yet keep the system in being.

Mrs. Butler did not fail to urge that the Commission had been appointed only to inquire into "the working and administration" of the Acts; while her contention was that the Acts in themselves were inconsistent with the spirit of the Constitution and law of Great Britain, which safeguards in the most solemn manner the personal freedom of the individual. She argued that twenty-five men sitting in a semi-private conference could not make a decision on the points in dispute, which must be submitted to the judgment of the whole nation, through their representatives in Parliament.

CHAPTER VII.

THE ROYAL COMMISSION OF 1870.

THE appointment of a Royal Commission to enquire into, and report upon, the Administration and Operation of the Acts must be considered in itself as a great triumph for Mrs. Butler and the principles she stood for ; and the findings of the Commission provided a still further triumph ; for the immediate discontinuance of compulsory examination and the abandonment of the virtual imprisonment of the suspected women were unanimously recommended ; and these two points constituted the very heart and essence of the C. D. Acts. The Repealers may very well have felt that in carrying the whole Commission with them in these points was a virtual triumph for their cause. I have always wondered why it was not hailed as such by the whole body who had followed Mrs. Butler's lead in resisting the Acts. Another extraordinary triumph was the conversion of an important group of the Commissioners from supporters to convinced opponents of the whole policy of the Acts. Among these converts were the following :

The Rev. F. D. Maurice who had signed a petition in favour of the Acts, relying on the judgment of some medical members of his congregation, became convinced of his error and as the evidence given before the Commission accumulated he published a full retraction, saying that the

Legislature, if it sanctioned these Acts, would put itself into hostility with the conscience of the nation.

Mr. Charles Buxton, M.P., who had entered the Commission as a Vice-President of a Society for the perpetuation of the Acts . . . " heard the evidence to its close, and then he ended his connection with the Society which favoured the Acts, and sent in a most energetic protest against their further maintenance." He also put on record a further protest, showing that so far from the Acts having done what was boasted of them they had been an utter failure and that voluntary hospitals had done more before the Acts were introduced than had been done since.

Sir Walter James in his recitation of the grounds of his objection to the Report as it stood, wrote : "All penal legislation upon the subject of the Contagious Diseases incident to prostitution seems to me to be productive of grave social injustice and immorality, and likely also to aggravate the grievous complaints which it is intended to cure."

It was also no small triumph for the Repealers to have obtained, through the appearance of Mr. J. S. Mill among the witnesses examined, clearly expressed and thoughtful pronouncements against these Acts from the leading philosophical statesman of the day. His answers to questions put to him by the Chairman at the very opening of his evidence contained the fullest corroboration of Mrs. Butler's principle : namely that the Acts were in direct violation of the principles of the Constitution and endangered the liberty not only of the women at whom the legislation was aimed, but of all women.

These were all important gains for the party of Repeal ; there was, however, another which calls for comment :

A paragraph in the main Report from which there had been no dissent ran as follows : " Traffic in children for infamous purposes is known to exist in notoriously considerable numbers in London and other large towns. We think a child of twelve can hardly be deemed capable of giving consent . . . We therefore recommend the absolute protection of female children to the age of 14 years, making the age of consent to commence at 14 instead of 12 years." It is grievous to remember that this very moderate recommendation was entirely ignored by the Government and Parliament ; and that it needed something like a social revolution in 1885, led by Mr. Stead in his paper the *Pall Mall Gazette*, to get the law altered and the age of consent raised to 16 years.

It was evident that the plan of the Government in framing the Royal Commission was to give approximately equal representation to both sides in the dispute, so that the resulting report might be a compromise rather than a triumph to either side. It was, therefore, not surprising that the report, when it finally appeared, was not without its inconsistencies ; for instance, the paragraph just quoted demanding a greater measure of protection for little girls of twelve years of age, reads strangely when compared with that which immediately followed. Alluding to a proposal which had been made in some quarters, not specified, that the men in the army and navy should also be subjected to these compulsory physical examinations, the report remarks paragraph 60, p. 17 : " *We may at once dispose of the recommendation, so far as it is founded on the principle of putting both parties . . . on the same footing, by the obvious but not less conclusive reply that there is no comparison to be made between prostitutes and the men who consort with them. With the one sex the offence is committed as a matter of gain ; with the other it is an irregular indulgence of a natural impulse.*" Considering that one party to the offence might be a child of twelve and the other a hardened old sinner of any age, it is almost inconceivable that sensible and experienced men could believe that invariably the woman (or in some cases, the child) was the more guilty of the two. Moreover, the wages women earned in some classes of industrial work were, at this time, so low that it was a grave question whether they sufficed for daily bread. But this is another instance of the ease of discriminating against the weaker side. It illustrates Mrs. Butler's wide vision combined with common sense that she so thoroughly realised how much moral evil arose out of the then low wage-earning powers of women.

It is strange now, after sixty years have passed, to read specimens of the vehemence with which many influential journals attacked the men and women who had devoted themselves to what they believed to be a sacred cause. The difference of tone between *Then* and *Now* is a measure of what the whole of society has gained from achieving a more dispassionate and reasonable view of the matter under discussion. Thus in July 1872, the *Times*, referring to Mr. Jacob Bright's speech against the Acts, omitted any report of it, merely stating that it was " entirely unfit for publication." Those who can recall his essentially refined and gentle nature can only stand amazed by such a statement. My own amazement has been in no degree weakened by reading the speech which was reported by Hansard. The *Saturday Review* of the period, out-Heroded Herod in its epithets and wrote in August 1872, of the " clamour of these *indecent maenads*," meaning the women who had been the chief opponents of the Acts.

Readers of the evidence given before the Royal Commission in 1870-1 will remember that some weighty recommendations made by witnesses who opposed the Acts, were to the effect that the Government and municipalities should afford free clinical attendance and advice to members of both sexes who voluntarily applied for them. Such a plan it was stated had been adopted with good results in Sweden. This plan was not even mentioned in the Report of the Royal Commission of 1871, but formed the chief constructive recommendation of the Commission which was created in 1913, and has been in operation ever since with amazingly good results as will be shown in our later pages.

The importance of the evidence of Mr. John Stuart Mill has just been mentioned. After a few preliminaries, descriptive of the legislation which had received the sanction of both Houses of Parliament, this question was asked by the Chairman:

" Do you consider that such legislation is justifiable in principle ? " To which his reply was (19,994) :

" I do not consider it justifiable in principle,
because it appears to me to be opposed to one of
the greatest principles of legislation, the security
of personal liberty. It appears to me that legislation of this sort takes away that security almost
entirely from a particular class of women inten-
tionally, but incidentally, and unintentionally, one
may say, for all women whatever ; inasmuch as it
enables a woman to be apprehended by the police
on suspicion and taken before a magistrate and
then by that magistrate she is liable to be confined
for a term of imprisonment, which may amount,
I believe, to six months, for refusing to sign a
declaration consenting to be examined."

In the latter part of his reply to a further question, Mr. Mill said (19,995) :

" But in any case it appears to me that we
ought not to assume, even supposing that no
case of abuse has been found out as yet, that
abuses will not occur. When power is given which
may easily be abused, we ought always to presume
that it will be abused ; and although it is possible
that great precaution will be taken at first, those
precautions are likely to be relaxed in time. We
ought not to give powers liable to very great abuse,
and easily abused, and then presume that those
powers will not be abused." The whole of Mill's
evidence, filling twenty-four pages of an octavo
pamphlet, emphasises this point of view, and is
identical with the spirit of English liberty. He,
furthermore, gave his reasons in detail why in
his view it was no part of the business of a Government to provide securities beforehand against the
consequences of immoralities of any kind. " That

is a totally different thing," he said, " from remedying the consequences after they occur. That I see no objection to at all. I see no objection to hospitals for the cure of patients, but I see considerable objections to consigning them to hospitals against their will."

Mr. Mill's evidence, with its candour and grasp of principle, must have considerably strengthened the case of the opponents of the Acts, and as has been shown, it was a confirmation, by the greatest political thinker of the age, of Mrs. Butler's contention that the Acts were a violation of the elementary principles of British law and custom.

When she gave her evidence it was soon perceived that the Commissioners were deeply impressed by it and especially by the contrast her whole demeanour and attitude of mind afforded to those of some of the promoters of the Acts. She, not alone, but above all others, gave an example of endeavouring to accept in all its bearings the teaching given by the Founder of Christianity on the equality of the sexes. "And the Scribes and Pharisees brought unto him a woman taken in adultery ; and when they had set her in the midst they say unto him : ' Master, this woman was taken in adultery. Now Moses in the law commanded that such should be stoned ; but what sayest thou ? ' . . . But Jesus stooped down and with his finger wrote on the ground as though he heard them not. So when they continued asking him, he lifted himself up and said unto them : ' He that is without sin among you, let him cast the first stone at her.' And again he stooped down and wrote on the ground. And they which heard

it being convicted by their own conscience went out one by one . . . and Jesus was left alone, and the woman standing in the midst. When Jesus had lifted himself and saw none but the woman, he said unto her : ' Woman, where are those thine accusers ? Hath no man condemned thee ? ' She said : ' No man, Lord.' And Jesus said : ' Neither do I condemn thee, go and sin no more.' ''
—John viii, 3-11.

Again when Mrs. Butler was giving evidence, she said, in reply to questions, that for fifteen years she had devoted her leisure to these unhappy women ; she had had five of them living in her house at one time, not as servants, but as friends and patients. She had sought them in brothels, night and day, in their homes and in the streets, in the Workhouses and in Lock Hospitals . . . '' Witness considered her labours successful in so far as the women became and remained virtuous, but for want of early industrial training they are difficult to suit with situations. The industrial question, she urged emphatically was all important.'' '' Economics,'' she argued, '' lie at the very root of practical morality.'' The want of industrial training and the want of good openings in the industrial world was one cause of their downfall, another was the crowding and want of decency in their homes. Asked whether women were willing to receive advice as to leading better lives she replied that '' the fallen women are always open to the sympathy and influence of those gifted by Providence with the art of reaching hearts.'' Asked to give a general idea as to the means by which the State might check profligacy, she replied that seduction might be punishable by law ; that legislation should deal equally with men and women and that the bastardy laws should be altered,* but she urged that the evil could not be reached by legislation alone, " the law must be aided by moral influences acting upon both men and women. There should be equal laws to check solicitation in the streets by either sex." She would never be satisfied by amendments in the Acts ; nothing would satisfy her but total repeal.

It will perhaps best convey the impression produced on the Commission by Mrs. Butler's evidence to quote verbatim what was said of it by one of the commissioners—Mr. Rylands. He wrote to a friend : " I am not accustomed to religious phraseology, but I cannot give you any idea of the effect produced except by saying that the influence of the Spirit of God was there."†

While the Royal Commission was receiving evidence and preparing its Report, the propaganda on behalf of repeal went steadily on. For the first time women began to take an active part in public affairs in spite of the opinion, held very generally at that time, that it was a disgraceful thing for any women even to appear on a public platform. Here were women not only organising and attending meetings in their thousands, but speaking on public platforms, and writing letters and pamphlets on a subject that public opinion was determined should not be mentioned. Of the effect of this new public opinion Mrs. Butler wrote :

* Several of these amendments of the law have been adopted since women became voters.
†Life of George Butler. p. 236.

" I have seen the system of Regulated Prostitution in all its varieties and forms ; I have
observed everywhere the stagnation of public
opinion so long as women have remained silent,
while in every country and place I have observed
the sudden inspiration of terror which seemed
to lay hold of the supporters of this evil institution, when they have perceived that they really
were about to encounter an active opposition
from women ; and I have become more than
ever convinced that systematised prostitution
will not be overthrown till it is attacked by
women, and at the same time that it cannot
resist that attack."

Even the women who did not speak, or go to
public meetings, or write pamphlets were so
stirred that they were prepared to put their signatures to public petitions in favour of repeal. On
April 6th, 1871, Mr. Duncan McLaren, M.P.,
and Mr. Candlish, M.P., presented a monster
petition to the House of Commons praying for the
Repeal of the Contagious Diseases Acts. The
petition contained 250,283 signatures. It was
received with laughter.

At that time, and for many years after, it was
the general habit of members of Parliament to
receive any mention of women, or of childbirth,
with roars of laughter.* It is worth something
to have stopped this. That sort of laughter is out
of fashion now.

* Mr. G. Bernard Shaw has called attention to the same indecent
hilarity which he met with several years ago when a member of a Health
Committee in one of the London boroughs. (*See* " New York Times,"
March 19, 1927.)

During 1870 and 1871, Mrs. Butler was writing and speaking continuously. She was the spearhead and the inspiration of the attack against the Acts, yet her indignation never degenerated into fanaticism, nor were her gaiety and sense of humour ever completely submerged in propaganda. Gradually she gathered round her the finest, bravest, noblest minds in Great Britain. Professor James Stuart, was already heart and soul in the movement, and in 1871, she was joined by Mr. and Mrs. Henry J. Wilson of Sheffield, who were from henceforth in the forefront of the struggle, bearing burdens and responsibility without ceasing. The same can be said of Mrs. Ford of Leeds, and the members of her family. Mrs. Butler gives in her account of the Pontefract bye-election of 1872 a thumb-nail sketch of Mr. Wilson which is at once graphic and revealing. It had been suggested that she should be escorted to the Town Hall, where she was to speak, by back streets, but some working men cried out : " No ! never go down by a back way. Come along through the middle of the crowd and before their (the opponents) windows ; we will protect you." " Our progress," adds Mrs. Butler, " was thus converted into a sort of triumphal procession, Mr. Wilson walking first with the Blue Book of the Royal Commission under his arm."

In addition to the National Association and the Ladies' National Association, both of which had headquarters in London, various other equally important Associations were formed for the repeal of the Acts. All these Associations raised their own funds, directed their own workers, and initiated various forms of propaganda and electoral activity. All worked in close conjunction with the London Societies and all of them looked to Mrs. Butler as their leader and drew inspiration from her unerring vision and unfaltering courage. The Country was covered by active associations such as the Northern Counties League ; the Midland Counties Electoral Association ; the North Eastern Association ; the Scottish National Association ; the Edinburgh and Glasgow Ladies' Committee, etc. Although Scotland was fortunately free from the operation of the Contagious Diseases Acts, the Scots people were quick to see that the system itself was a menace to liberty and many meetings of protest were held. At Glasgow, however, the University students attempted to break up a public meeting addressed by Mrs. Butler. The students were ejected and some of them were locked up for the night. " I asked," says Mrs. Butler, " one of the venerable Baillies to define the exact offence for which they had been locked up for the night, or fined. His reply was in broad Scotch, more racy, perhaps, than clearly judicial. ' They were punished,' he said, ' for the offence of barking like dogs, mewing like cats, crowing like cocks, whistling and rattling with their sticks.' "* In Ireland branches of the National and Ladies' National Associations were founded in Dublin, Cork and Belfast. Isabella Tod was the able and much beloved leader in the North of Ireland. A Medical League was formed to protest against the Acts and an important and influential Committee of the Free Churches was

* Personal Reminiscences.

founded with the same object. The Society of
Friends gave its support and encouragement to
Mrs. Butler's first public appeal and was ever
foremost in the struggle. In addition there is a
long list of individuals who helped the cause with
money or personal service. The battle was fought
from first to last by men and women, but from the
particular circumstances of the case and by reason
of the state of public opinion of that time, the
appearance of a woman as leader gave the struggle
a dramatic intensity which it would not otherwise
have possessed.

But it must not be forgotten that both for the
leader herself and the brave band of men and
women who followed her, those eventful years
meant a great deal in terms of personal sacrifice.
They were a group of great courage and of very
uncommon spiritual power. Their names are
recorded in the lists compiled by Mr. Benjamin
Scott in his book *The History of a State Iniquity*.
It is a list of which the Repealers may well be
proud. On p. 76 of *What I remember*, I have
mentioned a remark made to me by one of the
younger Fellows of Trinity Hall (my husband's
College), who said : " I don't know Stuart ; I
wish I did ; but I do know that when Middlemore
returns from seeing him he looks as if he had just
taken the Sacrament."

When one reflects that the Commission had
positively affirmed in 1871 the terrible facts of the
sale and purchase of children for " infamous
purposes " in London and other large towns, but
that nothing was done by Parliament to check and
prevent this until fourteen years later, when

W. T. Stead published his famous trumpet blast in the *Pall Mall Gazette*, it is not immaterial to remember that it was Mrs. Butler and Mr. Benjamin Scott, the City Chamberlain, who had urged Stead to take action. He, startled and bewildered by the revelations made to him, went to take counsel of the Head of the Criminal Investigation Department, at that time, Sir Howard Vincent. " Is it possible," said Stead, " that mothers in this very city would actually sell their children for infamous purposes ? " The reply was that it was perfectly possible, and that it had gone on unchecked for years and in any number of cases. Then Stead burst out : " It is enough to rouse Hell," and received the reply : " It does not even rouse the neighbours." But Sir Howard Vincent, and probably also Stead himself, were deceived. A new spirit was abroad, discernible in literature in this and other countries. It had roused Mrs. Browning to write *Aurora Leigh*. It had roused Dickens, when writing *David Copperfield*, to give the story of " Little Em'ly," and Steerforth, and of the heartbroken Peggotty and Ham. It had roused Meredith to give his version of the problem in *Rhoda Fleming ;* and above all it had roused Victor Hugo in *Les Misérables*, to reveal some of the villainies of the law and the possibility of the redemption of men and women by human compassion and faith. It was dawn breaking and not a false dawn.

W. T. STEAD.

Reproduced from " Review of Reviews " by kind permission of Mr. Wickham Steed.

CHAPTER VIII.

THE CAMPAIGN PROLONGED.

"If we could read the present as our successors will read it hereafter, we would thank God that we were born at such a time, and called to put our hands to a work which brings into exercise all the noblest qualities of the human mind and soul."—JOSEPHINE BUTLER.

IT is impossible to tell every detail of the long and arduous struggle against the Acts. The record is preserved in the Library of the Association for Moral and Social Hygiene, in the old volumes of the " Shield," in the " Story of a State Iniquity," by Benjamin Scott ; in " The Rough Record," an accurate and invaluable summary of the events compiled by Mr. Henry J. Wilson, and last but not least, in Mrs. Butler's " Personal Reminiscences of a Great Crusade." Agitation against the Acts was carried on in the teeth of extraordinary obstacles. The Press, with few exceptions was, after its first outburst in opposition to the Ladies' Manifesto, almost entirely silent. When the Repealers were not boycotted they were subjected to shameless misrepresentations and abuse. Nearly all authorities in Church and State, in Law and Medicine were definitely opposed to repeal, so that while there were, as we have seen, many individual members of Parliament, clergymen, lawyers, doctors and members of the Royal Commission of 1870 who were against the Acts, the general effect was a dead weight of opposition, which strengthened the public attitude of indifference and supported the Government in its refusal to repeal the Acts.

In spite of this dead weight of official opposition, the number of Repealers grew steadily, especially among working men and women who formed their own groups for propaganda and for obtaining signatures to their petitions for Repeal. Mrs. Butler was quick to appreciate the real value of these efforts. She writes in 1870 :

" When a very poor woman came to me with a single soiled petition sheet to be sent to the House of Commons, and I looked at the badly-written names which filled it, and heard her say : ' We held a little prayer-meeting, Ma'am, and all the women present signed it well knowing the meaning, and with all their hearts '—and when I read a heart-stirring memorial to a public man, penned by the trembling hand of a patient in hospital, fast bound by bodily infirmity, but broad in views and high in aims—I felt that an impulse had been given to the cause we have at heart, greater than is given perhaps by many an eloquent address, or scathing pamphlet, or the adhesion of some name great in the world's eyes."

An incident from a bye-election at Pontefract in 1871 is typical of the enthusiasm and self-regardless effort that her words could arouse in the hearts and minds of men. A working man of Leeds walked over to Pontefract a distance of twenty miles, after his day's work, solely for the pleasure of helping the Repealers by the distribution of leaflets and papers to the electorate, though well aware, that, in order to be at work again next day, he must travel the return journey, also on foot. Thus he tramped forty miles between leaving work at night and starting again next morning.

The supporters of the Acts could draw on no such devotion but they could sometimes buy or incite a mob to deeds of violence as the following account of a meeting at the same bye-election proves. Mrs. Butler writes :

" On a certain afternoon, when Mr. Childers, the Government candidate, was again to address a large meeting from the window of a house, I and my lady friends determined to hold a meeting at the same hour, thinking we should be unmolested. We had to go all over the town before we found anyone bold enough to let us a place to meet in. At last, we found a large hayloft over an empty room on the outskirts of the town. You could only ascend to it by means of a kind of ladder, leading through a trap-door in the floor. However, the place was large enough to hold a good meeting, and soon filled. Stuart had run on in advance and paid for the room in his own name, and looked in to see that all was right. He found the floor strewn with cayenne pepper to make it impossible for us to speak, and there were some bundles of straw in the empty room below. He got a poor woman to help him and with buckets of water he managed to drench the floor and sweep together the cayenne pepper. Still, when we arrived, it was very unpleasant for eyes and throat. We began our meeting with prayer, and the women were listening,

with increasing determination never to forsake
the good cause, when a smell of burning was
felt, smoke began to curl up through the floor,
and a threatening noise was then heard under-
neath at the door. The bundles of straw
beneath had been set on fire, and the smoke
much annoyed us. To our horror, looking
down the room to the trap-door entrance, we
saw head after head appear ; man after man
came in, until they crowded the place. There
was no possible exit for us, the windows being
high above the ground, and we were gathered
into one end of the room like a flock of sheep
surrounded by wolves. They were mostly *not*
Yorkshire people ; they were led on by two
or three *gentlemen* (?) one of them became
afterwards a candidate for Parliament.
'' It would hardly do to describe in words what
followed. It was a time which required strong
faith and calm courage. Mrs. Wilson and I
stood in front of the company of women, side
by side. She whispered in my ear : ' Now is
the time to trust in God ; don't let us fear.'
And a wonderful sense of the Divine presence
came to us both. You understand, it was not
so much personal violence that we feared, as
what would have been to any of us worse than
death ; for the indecencies of the men, their
gestures and threats, were what I would prefer
not to describe. Their language was hideous.
They shook their fists in our faces, with volleys
of oaths. This continued for some time, and
we had no defence or means of escape. Their
chief rage was directed against me ; half a

dozen fists were in my face at once, and the
epithets applied were such as one only hears
of in brothels. They filled their foul talk with
allusions to the ' visites ' under the Contagious
Diseases Acts, with which they all seemed
minutely familiar. It was very clear that they
understood that ' their craft was in danger.'
The new teaching and revolt of women had
stirred up the very depths of hell. We said
nothing, for our voices could not have been
heard. We simply stood shoulder to shoulder
—Mrs. Wilson and I—and waited and endured.
But it seemed all the time as if some strong
angel were present, for when these men's
hands were literally upon us, they seemed held
back by some unseen power. There was a
young Yorkshire woman, strong and stalwart,
with bare arms, and a shawl over her head,
among our flock behind us. She dashed forward
and fought her way through the crowd of men,
and escaped down the ladder, and, running
as hard as she could, she found Mr. Stuart
on the outskirts of Mr. Childers' meeting,
and said to him : ' Come ! run ! they are
killing Mrs. Butler.' He did run, and came
up the ladder stairs into the midst of the
crowd. As soon, however, as they perceived
that he was our defender, they were down on
him. A strong man seized him in his arms ;
another opened the window, and they were
going to throw him headlong out. I ran forward
between him and the window. This was
enough to give him time to slip cleverly from
between the man's arms on to the floor and

glide away to the side where we were. He
then asked to be allowed to say a few words to
them, and with good temper and coolness, he
argued that he had taken the room, that it was
his, and if they would kindly let the ladies go,
he would hear what they had to say. A fierce
argument began. Meanwhile, stones were
thrown into the windows, and broken glass
flew across the room. While all this was going
on (it seemed to us like hours of horrible
endurance), hope came at last, in the shape of
two or three helmeted policemen, whose heads
appeared one by one up through the trap-door.
Now, we thought, we are safe ! But no ! These
Metropolitans had been hired by the Government, and they simply looked at the scene
for a few moments with a cynical smile, and
left the place without an attempt to defend us.
My heart grew sick as I saw them disappear.
It seemed now to become desperate.
" Mrs. Wilson and I whispered to each other
in the midst of the din : ' Let us ask God to
help us, and make a rush for the entrance.'
Two or three Yorkshire working women put
themselves in the front, and we pushed our
way I don't know how, to the stairs. It was
only myself and one or two other ladies that
the men really cared to do violence to ; so if
we could get away, the rest would be all right.
I made a dash forward and took one flying leap
from the trap door on to the ground floor
below. It was a long jump, but, being light,
I came down all right. I was not a bit too soon,
for the feet of the men were ready to kick my

head as it disappeared down the hole. I found Mrs. Wilson after me very soon in the street. Once in the street, of course, these cowards did not dare to offer us the same violence. We went straight to our own hotel, and there we had a magnificent women's meeting. Such a revulsion of feeling came over the inhabitants of Pontefract when they heard of this disgraceful scene, that they flocked to hear us, many of the women weeping. We had to turn the lights low, and close the windows for fear of the mob; but the hotel was literally crowded with women, and we scarcely needed to speak—events had spoken for us, and all honest hearts were won."

—Personal Reminiscences.

In 1872 the Government seemed to have become seriously alarmed at the strides the Repeal movement was making throughout the country. It could hardly set up another Royal Commission of Enquiry; but it introduced into Parliament a measure known afterwards as " Bruce's Bill," which yielded certain points that the Repealers had contended for, but left the general tenour of the law Regulationist in effect. Whether or not as many of the Repealers believed this Bill was deliberately intended by the Government to sow dissension in the ranks of the Repealers, and reduce them to two factions contending with one another is not now, and probably never was, susceptible of proof. But as a matter of fact it very nearly did have this result, for to many Repealers it seemed that the Bill offered so much of what they asked that it ought to be accepted. But Mrs. Butler refused all compromise, and though at first only a few stood with her, she was prepared to risk all that had been won, estrange many of her supporters, and break up her party rather than accept the Bill. She wrote :

" It (Mr. Bruce's Bill) was so skilfully, I may say, so craftily, framed and contained so many positive measures for the protection of the weak and the moralising of the vicious, that it was calculated to deceive, as it were, the very elect of our ranks.

" A meeting was held in London to consider this Bill. There were several delegates of our League from all parts of the country. A long discussion took place, several members of Parliament spoke, and it was at last agreed that there was so much good in this Bill that it ought to be accepted by us as an instalment, upon which they hoped would follow something more thorough. The question was put to the meeting, and a resolution was voted, apparently unanimously, that the Bill should be accepted. I heard a whisper behind me, and looking round I saw two pale women (two of my earliest fellow workers) who had not held up their hands (even as I had not) in favour of the acceptance of this measure. I went near them and we whispered to each other that such acceptance would be the ruin of our cause and we asked each other : ' What shall we do ? ' One of the group then stood up and said there were three women there who objected.

" The President of the meeting, the late Professor Francis Newman, a man who had a profound respect for womanhood, gave a deep sigh, almost a groan, and said : ' Gentlemen, we must pause ! If only one intelligent woman should object to the acceptance of this Bill, we must reconsider the whole matter, and hear what she has to say.' This note produced a feeling of consternation in the meeting. Two men, however, our most faithful adherents, came at once to our side. The meeting ended in confusion, but almost all who were present had virtually accepted the Government project . . ."

" There followed many weeks of sad feeling of isolation, and separation from the great bulk of our former adherents ; but during those weeks a few of us were silently working and bringing to bear upon the various clauses the principles of British Constitutional Law. We read, we studied, we thought, we prayed, as it were, for our very lives. We published our papers and our books and disseminated them."

The result was that the Goverment withdrew their Bill, and, to quote Mrs. Butler again :

" In course of time the truth prevailed, and almost to a man all those who had wavered came forward, and were more firmly established than before in the principles of our cause ; but this result did not come about at once, but slowly one by one, or in small groups. And so we learned hope for the erring, and patience under delays and disappointments."

—Personal Reminiscences.

This was a severe test for the Repeal movement ; it was ultimately the source of new strength. It emerged from the ordeal strong, firm, united, determined never again to compromise till the victory was won. From 1872 to 1886 it settled down to hard dogged work, in Parliament and in the country. Year after year a repeal Bill was introduced into Parliament ; year after year, meetings were held, petitions were signed, statistics were collected. Evidence was sought and weighed, pamphlets and leaflets and the weekly issue of the " Shield " published and sent out far and wide. Year by year public prejudice was broken down ; year by year the number of convinced repealers grew in numbers and voting strength ; year by year the truth about the ghastly failure of Regulation, not only in this country but in France and other countries was brought home to the mind and heart of the general public. It was a slow and laborious work, but it was built on a solid foundation of principle, justice and fact, and after 1872 the movement never really looked back, though there were times of deep depression when little or no progress seemed visible, for it cannot be denied that the opponents of the Acts during the next few years were going through a time, not of doubt or hesitation, but of discouragement. There was no sign in Parliament of any serious intention on the part of the Government, or of private members, to introduce legislation giving legal effect to the recommendations of the Royal Commission or even to raise the age of protection for girls. Such a Bill had been drafted and had been successfully piloted through a Committee of the House of Lords and finally through the Upper Chamber itself by the good Lord Shaftesbury ; but this Bill, session after session, was destroyed in the

House of Commons, being talked out, counted out, or otherwise defeated by means familiar to old parliamentary hands.

In 1874 the Liberals were defeated at a General Election and a Conservative Government was returned to power, a fact which made Parliamentary work very difficult for the Repealers. Otherwise 1874 was remarkable for two things, the inauguration of Abolitionist work on the Continent,* and the public adherence of the Rt. Hon. James Stansfeld, set free by the defeat of Mr. Gladstone's Government, in which he had held office, to devote his whole strength to the cause of Repeal. Mr., afterwards Sir James, Stansfeld's declaration, made at a Meeting of the Ladies' National Association at Bristol, created a deep impression, for he was a public man who had held many important posts, who had been President of the Local Government Board in the late Liberal Government and was greatly esteemed. His speech was deemed of such importance that it broke down the conspiracy of silence adopted by the greater part of the Press. This adherence was a great gain not only because Mr. Stansfeld was held in such regard by the general public but also on account of his Parliamentary knowledge and standing which was henceforth entirely devoted to the repeal of the Acts. Mrs. Butler wrote enthusiastically of the immense accession of strength to her cause received from his support, and W. T. Stead expressed himself on the same subject in a characteristic vein. " It was," he wrote, " an odious

* In order not to interrupt the continuity of the narrative here, the work in Europe, India, America and the Colonies will be described in a future chapter.

duty from which all Right Honourables had
hitherto shrunk. Right Honourables there were
in plenty who voted for and enforced the Acts,
from Mr. Gladstone downwards. Right Honourables who would risk reputation, position,
career for a cause, such as this, there was only
one, and his name was Stansfeld . . . Mr. Stansfeld
had however, caught from Mazzini, with whom
he had lived for many years in closest intimacy,
something of that divine thirst for self-sacrifice
which enables men, even when they have sat in
Cabinets, to give up all and follow the supreme call
of Duty and Pity."

Josephine Butler

CHAPTER IX.

THE REPEAL OF THE ACTS.

"Injustice is immoral, oppression is immoral, the sacrifice of the interests of the weaker to the stronger is immoral, and all these immoralities are embodied in all systems of legalised prostitution, in whatever part of the world or under whatever title they exist."
—JOSEPHINE BUTLER.

IN 1879 the Conservative Government appointed yet another Select Committee of the House of Commons to report on the working of the Contagious Diseases Acts. This Committee took evidence during 1880, 1881 and 1882. Its report was issued in 1882, and consisted of a majority report signed by nine members and a minority report signed by six members. The two medical members took opposite sides.

This prolonged inquiry by the Select Committee, whilst it did not prevent the progress of the agitation in the country hampered and frustrated Parliamentary action during those years, as the Government may very probably have intended that it should do.

It will be remembered that in 1864 when the first C. D. Act was introduced, the medical profession as a whole, were, throughout Europe, in favour of regulation of prostitution. It was almost universally considered by doctors and administrators alike to be the only method of dealing with the physical evils caused by prostitution. But the continual propaganda of the Repealers both in this country and abroad was beginning to bear fruit. Moreover, extended experience was beginning to prove beyond a doubt that the supposed safety promised by the supporters of the Acts was entirely fictitious. In August, 1881, an International Medical Congress was held in London. This Congress afforded an excellent opportunity for discussing Regulation under the heading of State Medicine, and medical men of the highest European eminence attended the meeting. Papers had been announced by Dr. Gihon, the Medical Director of the United States Navy, and Dr. Bellem of Lisbon, who were both strongly regulationist and advocates of the general adoption of stringent methods of control applied to the whole civil population. Dr. Gihon did not appear, but he sent a paper which was read at the Congress, and was strangely moderate in tone. Dr. Bellem neither appeared nor sent his paper. Professor Henry Lee, Dr. Drysdale, and Dr. Allbut read papers which exposed the futility of Regulation in a masterly fashion, and in the ensuing discussion all the weight of argument was in favour of the opponents of the Acts. At former International Congresses strong resolutions had been carried in favour of extending the regulation system. At this Congress no attempt was made even to propose a resolution in favour of the system, a striking testimony to the growing influence of Repeal propaganda.

Another powerful aid was Mrs. Butler's courageous exposure in 1880 of the traffic in children

between London and Belgium. On May 1, 1880,
she published a statement in England concerning
this traffic. Her accusations were based on her
own observations and the investigations of two
Quakers, Mr. Alfred Dyer and Mr. George Gillett.
Her statement which was reprinted in the French,
Belgian and Italian newspapers, was received with
indignation and incredulity. Perhaps it is difficult
for us to realise the state of public opinion on these
questions in 1880 ; certainly many people would
then have preferred that the hideous thing should
go on rather than it should be dragged to the
light and exposed. Even those who believed in Mrs.
Butler trembled at her audacity, and many begged
her to withdraw her statements and be silent
on this subject. One of her supporters in Brussels
wrote to an English friend : " Do you know that
you are walking into the jaws of hell ? " But
hell had no terrors for this heroic woman who
went through the world on fire against injustice
and slavery. The Belgian authorities challenged
her to prove her statements and to make a deposition on oath. The English authorities were un-
sympathetic, if not hostile, and attempts were
made to intimidate her. But she persevered and
the deposition was made in the room of the Chief
Magistrate of Liverpool in November. Mrs.
Butler writes :

" I made my deposition in the month of
November, in the room of the Chief Magistrate.
There were present, besides my husband, half
a dozen of the most solid and honourable citizens
of Liverpool, who were deeply interested in
the whole matter, my Counsel, Dr. Commins

and a reporter. My deposition was forwarded to Sir William Harcourt (then Home Secretary in Gladstone's administration), and by him to the Procureur du Roi, at Brussels. From that time forward there were no more attempts to deny the charges I had made. The proofs of everything I had said were too strong to be set aside, while Mr. Dyer's action, and the facts cited in my deposition, produced results in Belgium for which all the friends of Justice were thankful."*

Some months later she sent a copy of her deposition to the Editor of a well-known Brussels paper. She did not intend this for publication but simply for the Editor's information ; nevertheless he did publish it and it made as great a sensation in Brussels as it had done in London. One consequence was the dismissal of the Brussels Chief of the *Police des Moeurs* which was followed by the resignation of his principal subordinates. Another consequence was the formation of a strong Committee in London for the suppression of the White Slave Traffic ; and this brought the late Mr. W. A. Coote into the work and led a few years later to his appointment as secretary of the National Vigilance Association, a position in which he did invaluable work ; for it was largely by his efforts, backed by his knowledge, that the Governments of Europe, represented at the Assembly of the League of Nations in 1921, were induced to sign an International Convention for the suppression of the traffic in women and children.

*Personal Reminiscences.

All this was to the good, especially in spreading knowledge of the facts and rousing public opinion. But Mrs. Butler, though of course warmly in sympathy with Mr. Coote's efforts, did not fail to point out that there is a grave risk, in those countries where the authorities themselves license immoral houses, that the police will not and cannot honestly and thoroughly endeavour to prevent the traffic upon which the profits of those houses so largely depend. This, it must be remembered, was more than forty years before the same subject was taken up by the League of Nations in 1921, when a strongly worded Convention was adopted by the Assembly in that year. Mrs. Butler and her colleagues in 1880 had sowed the seed which bore such good fruit in 1921, and is still bearing fruit in the Report issued by the League of Nations of the *Special Body of Experts on the Traffic in Women and Children*. When this Report made its appearance in February, 1927, many of her old colleagues must have said in their hearts: " She being dead yet speaketh."

In 1880 similar revelations, in spite of official efforts to hush them up, came from France and other European countries and created a stir of public indignation. In England the cause of the children was taken up by Mr. W. T. Stead, who published a series of articles called " The Maiden Tribute " in the *Pall Mall Gazette*, in 1885. Mr. Stead's generous and impulsive heart was profoundly moved by Mrs. Butler's revelations concerning the continued " sale of children for infamous purposes " which had been denounced by the

Royal Commission of 1871 ; but this had not succeeded in rousing Parliament to amend the law for their further protection. On the contrary the man who had attempted to provide further protection for them was charged with criminal conspiracy and for co-operation with another to disregard the sacred right of the father to the possession of the child, and on this charge Mr. Stead was condemned in 1885 to six months imprisonment as an ordinary offender.* No first-class treatment was allowed him, and in mid-November he wore cotton prison clothes in a cold cell, until his friends were successful in obtaining for him the treatment of a first-class misdemeanant.   He bore the whole thing not only with cheerfulness but with gaiety, gloried in his prison dress which he asked, and I believe obtained, leave to retain in his own possession as a souvenir of his imprisonment. He published the whole story of his " conspiracy " and the events which had led up to it. A rather interesting feature of the disclosures which were made about that time was that the " injured father " from whose care the child had been " abducted " without his consent, was not, in law, the father at all, as the child had been born out of wedlock. According to the lying legal phrase she was a *filius nullius*. Mrs. Butler also published her first-hand knowledge of the case which had led up to Stead's imprisonment.   These pamphlets, coupled with Stead's joyful acceptance of the unjust sentence passed upon him roused public interest in the highest

* See note at end of Chapter, p. 106.

degree and were a source of great strength to the rapidly growing party in the country who were demanding the total repeal of the C. D. Acts. It also led to a very considerable revision of the Criminal Law Amendment Act in 1886. It should never be forgotten, in justification of the sensational action that had been taken, that although the Royal Commission on the C. D. Acts in 1871 had reported unanimously in favour of raising the age of the protection of girls, Parliament had done nothing whatever to carry this recommendation into effect until Stead caused it to reconsider its ways. I know I have said this already, but it cannot be rubbed in too much.

In 1883 Josephine Butler published the story of the persecution of the Salvation Army in Switzerland. The keepers of the State-protected houses of ill-fame in Geneva were up in arms against the Salvationists ; and like the sellers of trophies from the shrines of Diana in Ephesus, some 1,800 years earlier, fearing their hopes of gain were threatened, they secured bands of roughs who disturbed the Army meetings and caused scenes of violence and disorder. Miss Catherine Booth and Miss Charlesworth were expelled from Geneva, first from the city and a little later from the Canton. But the persecution did their cause good rather than harm ; and these strange events—the spectacle of the City of Calvin identifying itself with the keepers of bad houses and expelling the Salvationists—came as near a farce as was within the bounds of possibility. The people for whom Milton's magnificent sonnet " Avenge, O Lord thy slaughtered saints," was written, must have strangely changed before they could become the persecutors of the Salvation Army and the protectors of licensed houses of ill-fame.

All these events made for publicity and publicity was that which was most dreaded by the *souteneurs* and *tenanciers* of Geneva. (I am glad there is no English name for them.) The events just recorded made a noise not merely in Geneva but all over Europe. In England, especially, they threw light on Mrs. Butler's work which had been but little perceived in earlier years. One needs constantly to remind oneself that the more decent and well-doing the ordinary man is, the less he knows or hears of the dark deeds of the underworld. But the horrors just referred to had made a great stir, and the constituencies began to take the matter up. There had been a General Election in 1880, and it had been an election under a further extension of the franchise ; for there was, from this year onwards, household suffrage for men, in counties as well as in boroughs. One of the first results of this was that the operations of the C. D. Acts were suspended in 1883, though their actual repeal was not carried until 1886.

The story must now be continued from Mrs. Butler's own narrative. She wrote personal letters, which she afterwards permitted to be published, in February 1883, describing what was taking place. She and her husband had spent the previous weekend at Cambridge to enjoy the rest and refreshment of a quiet Sunday. Mr. Stuart, not yet in Parliament, was their host while in Cambridge : they met there an M.P., who spoke of the tremendous pressure being brought to bear on members

to secure the rejection of the Acts ; it was, he
thought, unprecedented in the history of any
agitation. " Our friends," he said, " are active
in every nook and corner of the country ; even
from remote villages petitions come pouring in,
as well as many single petitions from such leaders
as Cardinal Manning and the Moderator of the
Free Church of Scotland. Mr. Hopwood (an
M.P. very honourably distinguished for his leading
part in the House and country against the Acts)
told us that several M.P.s ' came to him yesterday
and said they must vote with us, though before
they had been hostile.' ' It is a strange thing,'
said one, ' that people care so much about this
question. All my leading constituents have asked
me to vote with you.' One of our strongest
opponents, a military man, said to me : ' well you
have extraordinary support from the country. It is
evident that yours is the winning side.' "

Mrs. Butler, continuing her narrative a little
later, wrote : " There is a distinct change of tone
in the House, and we believe it dates from the
time when we came forward to claim God as
our Leader. Our cause was openly baptised, so
to speak, in the name of Christ and our advance
has been steady ever since. Also I thought I saw
what I had never observed before, in the sceptical
and worldly atmosphere of Parliament, *i.e.*, signs
of a consciousness of a spiritual strife going on.
Some members spoke to us of the spiritual power
in our movement, while on the other hand there is
a seething and boiling of unworthy passions, such
as would appal one if one did not remember that
it was when the great Incarnation of purity drew

near to the possessed men of old that the unclean spirits cried out . . ." " We have arranged for a great meeting for prayer. We shall hold it close to the House of Commons during the whole Debate and all night if the Debate lasts all night . . ."

Continuing her narrative she wrote : " February 28, 1883. We went to the House at four o'clock yesterday . . . I did not remain in the Ladies' Gallery but came and went from the Prayer meeting to the Lobby of the House. We saw John Morley take the oath and his seat. The first thing he did after taking the oath was to sit down by Mr. Hopwood and say : " Now tell me what I can do to help you to-night, for the thing our Newcastle electors were most persistent about was that I should oppose this legislation.* I then went to the Westminster Palace Hotel where we had taken a large room for our devotional meeting. There were well-dressed ladies . . . kneeling together (almost side by side) with the poorest and some of the outcast women of the purlieus of Westminster. Many were weeping, but when I went in first they were singing. I never heard a sweeter sound . . . I felt ready to cry but I did not ; for I had long ago rejected the old ideal of the division of labour ' that men must work and women must weep ' . . . " " A venerable lady from America rose and said : ' Tears are good, prayers are better, but we should get on better if

*One of John Morley's most influential and valued supporters in his recent election had been Dr. Spence Watson. He, and likewise his wife, were devoted adherents of Mrs. Butler's policy. In after years, Morley, discussing with friends the meaning of the words " the beauty of holiness," said he had never understood what they meant until he became acquainted with Mrs. Spence Watson.

behind every tear there was a vote at the ballot box.*
Every soul in that room responded to the senti-
ment ; I never saw a meeting more moved.

" Mr. Hopwood's motion did not come up
for division on that evening, being pressed out by
other business ; but he made a good speech
rather to the country than to the House, explaining
how he was prevented from bringing in
his resolution. Mr. (afterwards Sir George)
Trevelyan told Mrs. Butler he thought our
opponents had purposely prolonged the debate
on the Address to prevent Mr. Hopwood's motion
from coming on." Mrs. Butler mentions also in
her letters how her husband's friends and old
pupils had gathered round her in the Lobby, with
words of cheer and encouragement, especially
mentioning Albert Grey, afterwards Earl Grey, and
Robert Reid, afterwards Lord Loreburn.

On April 20th Mr. Stansfeld moved his resolution condemning compulsory examination ; this
was identical with the one which Mr. Hopwood
had been prevented moving in February, and was
as follows :

" That this House disapproves of the compulsory examination of women under the Contagious Diseases Acts."

* These prophetic words have been amply justified by events. To
take only one instance : before women had the vote the Bastardy Act
of 1872 fixed the sum of 5s. a week as the maximum which a father,
whatever his wealth, could be made to pay towards the maintenance of
an illegitimate child. In 1918 as soon as women were enfranchised,
without any trouble or agitation Parliament increased this sum to 10s.
a week, and in 1923 a new Bastardy Act was passed which raised the
maximum to 20s. a week. (*See* pamphlet issued in 1925, entitled : " *What
the Vote has Done*," published by the National Union of Societies for
Equal Citizenship, 15, Dean's Yard, S.W.1. This publication was origin-
ally a single page leaflet ; it has now grown to a six-page pamphlet, and
has to be constantly enlarged.)

" There was a great muster of members, the Strangers' Gallery, the Speaker's Gallery, and the Lobbies were crowded. Mr. Stansfeld, speaking amidst a scene of intense excitement, made a speech which deeply impressed the House, and his motion was carried by 182 votes to 110. It was the Repealers first Parliamentary victory, and it was a magnificent one ; for it meant, as the Pro-Act party were quick to realise, that regulation had received its death blow in Great Britain."

Mrs. Butler has described the scene within the House of Commons in a letter to her sister, Madame Meuricoffre, from which we quote :

WINCHESTER, April, 1883.
" Some day I trust I shall be able to tell you in detail of the events of the last few days. I longed for your presence during the debate ; it was for us a very solemn time. All day long groups had met for prayer—some in the houses of M.P.s, some in churches, some in halls, where the poorest people came. Meetings were being held also all over the kingdom, and telegraphic messages of sympathy came to us continually from Scotland, and Ireland, France and Switzerland and Italy. There was something in the air like the approach of victory. As men and women prayed they suddenly burst forth into praise, thanking God for the answer, as if it had already been granted. It was a long debate. The tone of the speeches, both for and against, was remarkably purified, and with one exception they were altogether on a higher plane than in former debates. Many of us ladies sat through the whole evening

till after midnight; then came the division.
A few minutes previously Mr. Gerald, the
steward of the Ladies' Gallery, crept quietly
in and whispered to me, ' I think you are
going to win ! ' That reserved official, of
course, never betrays sympathy with any party,
nevertheless, I could see the irrepressible
pleasure in his face when he said this.

" Never can I forget the expression on the
faces of our M.P.s in the House when they
all streamed back from the division Lobby.
The interval during their absence had seemed
very long, and we could hear each other's
breathing, so deep was the silence. We did not
require to wait to hear the announcement
of the division by the tellers : the faces of
our friends told the tale. Slowly and steadily
they pressed in, headed by Mr. Stansfeld and
Mr. Hopwood, the tellers on our side. Mr.
Fowler's face was beaming with joy and a
kind of humble triumph. I thought of the
words : " Say unto Jerusalem that her warfare
is accomplished." It was a victory of righteousness over great selfishness, injustice and deceit,
and for the moment we were all elevated by it.
When the figures were given out a long-
continued cheer arose, which sounded like a
psalm of praise. Then we ran quickly down
from the gallery, and met a number of our
friends coming from Westminster Hall.

" It was half-past one in the morning, and the
stars were shining in the clear sky. I felt at that
silent hour in the morning in the spirit of the
Psalmist, who said : ' When the Lord turned

again the captivity of Sion we were like unto them that dream.' It almost seemed like a dream.

" When Mr. Cavendish Bentinck was speaking against us I noticed an expression of pain on Mr. Gladstone's face. He seemed to be pretending to read a letter, but at last passed his hand over his eyes and left the House. He returned before Mr. Stansfeld made his noble speech, to which he listened attentively." *J.J.*

As a result of this Parliamentary victory the operation of the Acts was immediately suspended. Actual repeal, however, was retarded and the Repealers felt that a strenuous effort must be made to gain the final victory. There was a General Election in 1885 and great efforts were made to obtain pledges from all candidates in favour of complete repeal. A large number of repeal candidates were elected and on March 16th, 1886, Mr. Stansfeld moved the following resolution :

" That in the opinion of this House the Contagious Diseases Acts, 1868 and 1869 ought to be repealed."

An amendment was defeated by a majority of 114, and the motion was then carried without a division. On March 18th, Mr. Stansfeld introduced his Repeal Bill. It went through all its stages in the House of Commons, and was introduced in the House of Lords on April 5th. The third reading was on April 13th, and on April 15th it received the Royal Assent. This victory was the culminating triumph of Mrs. Butler's life. Sir James Stansfeld and Mr. Stuart sent a telegram to Mr. and Mrs. Butler who were in Italy : " Royal

Assent has this day been given to the Repeal Bill."
No one but the possessor of extraordinary
spiritual power could have won such a victory.
Such power was in the most eminent degree
Mrs. Butler's. Hardly anyone could come in
contact with her without feeling it ; and I hope I
am not presumptous when in my own mind, I
apply to her, words that were spoken by and of
Another : " This sort goeth not forth but by
prayer and fasting."
The victory of the Repealers in this country
was complete. Not only did it erase from the
constitution a cruel and worthless Act of Parliament, but the long years of propaganda had been
invaluable, not only on the question of the repeal
of the Acts, but in shedding light on the wider
aspect of women's place as responsible citizens
in the body politic. When Parliament repealed
the Contagious Diseases Acts, it did so supported by
the full weight of an informed public opinion. The
steadily accumulating pressure of facts and statistics
from all parts of the world proving the utter
inadequacy of the system to prevent disease or
suppress prostitution, had had its effect. In England
in 1886, people knew the Regulation system for
what it was, arbitrary, unjust and cruel to the
women concerned ; and a wholly illusory safe-
guard for their partners. In the following chapters
it will be related how the struggle passed on to
Europe, India, America, and the Colonies. Mrs.
Butler had no intention of abandoning the fight
against Regulation. She wrote from Winchester
in 1886 :
" I am very anxious to make the forthcoming

The Life and Work of

Congress of the Federation worthy of the occasion. We have just obtained a great victory; but we have still to destroy the accursed system in the whole range of our Empire beyond the seas; and we have to help our Continental neighbours. So long as the State protects prostitution, this dreadful international slave traffic will go on; and we English will suffer by it. Our Abolitionist public has to some extent been quieted by Repeal; and it is not so easy to raise them up again."

Note to page 96.

It should always be remembered with gratitude to the Salvation Army that it was their General, Bramwell Booth, who put Stead in possession of the facts which he made public in July, 1885, with regard to the then almost wholly unchecked traffic in little children "for infamous purposes." These horrors, published in a well-known and popular paper, made a tremendous sensation, not only in England, but throughout the world. The Powers of Darkness furiously raged together and promised themselves, "if not victory at least revenge." Stead and the General, with some others were prosecuted at the Old Bailey on the charge of unlawfully taking a young girl under 13 from the possession of her father without his consent. The trial lasted 13 days, ending on November 8th, with the result that the General was acquitted but Stead was condemned as stated. He had obtained the consent of the mother, but had not even sought the consent of the father; the Judge (Mr. Justice Lopez) ruled that " the consent of the mother was nothing, that the consent of her father was everything." The jury added a rider to their verdict to the effect that they wished to put on record " their high appreciation of the services Mr. Stead had rendered the nation by securing the passage of a much needed law for the protection of young girls." (See *Life of W. T. Stead*, by Mr. Frederic Whyte. pp. 1845, Vol. 1, and *Echoes and Memories*, by Bramwell Booth. Chapter XIV.)

CHAPTER X.

WORK ABROAD.

"That we are, and have been all along, contending for more than the mere repeal of these unjust and unholy Acts of Parliament, is proved by certain signs, which are becoming more and more frequent. We were, perhaps, ourselves unconscious, some of us are probably yet unconscious, how great is the undertaking upon which we have entered."—JOSEPHINE BUTLER.

IN 1873 the International Medical Congress, at its meeting in Vienna, had reaffirmed the opinion that State Regulation was the only method of dealing with the diseases accompanying prostitution, and they demanded an international and administrative law in order to widen the scope and increase the severity of Regulation. This evidence of the determination on the part of the Regulationists to strengthen their position, together with the growing conviction in the minds of the English Repealers that there would be no quick or easy victory for their cause in England, made them take stock of the whole position. Mrs. Butler, who had travelled widely on the Continent and studied the working of the system in various great cities for herself, was convinced that a world-wide attack was necessary. A Conference was held therefore, at York, on June 25th, 1874, to discuss the whole position. This Conference laid on Mrs. Butler the task of challenging public opinion in Europe. She left for Paris in December, 1874,

and her first act was to seek an interview with
M. Lecour, the Chief in Paris of the *Police des
Moeurs*. Nothing could more efficiently illustrate
the strength of the missionary spirit which animated
her. She had this spirit as strongly as St. Paul
himself. She said, in part humourously, that
she did feel as she faced Lecour " rather like
Paul before Nero." She was struck by his richly
appointed office, his sumptuous furniture, and his
retinue of liveried servants. One of her first
questions to him was to enquire : " If vice and
disease were diminished in Paris during the
last five years ? " He must have been rather
a stupid man since he appeared to miss the drift
of her question, his reply being a virtual confession of the uselessness of his system ; for he
answered promptly : " Oh, no, increased ; they
go always increasing, continually increasing " ;
and when she asked him to what he attributed this
increase and if he had been so long at his Pre-
fecture without it occurring to him that the men,
for whose health he laboured and for whom he
enslaved women, were guilty in the same sense as
women, he became agitated and excited, and when
she tried to bring him back to his confession of the
hygienic uselessness of his system, he shrugged
his shoulders and said : " Who hopes for great
hygienic results ? " " Those," she replied, " belong,
I suppose, to the region of romance."

In a letter to her sister, Mme. Meuricoffre,
she gives an account of this interview with
Lecour, and describes the impression he made
upon her as that of a " shallow, vain and talkative
man " ; and she mentions how though it was

a grey cloudy day, she suddenly saw through an open window " a speck of blue sky," and she adds that she " held on to that speck," all through the rest of the interview.*

I too, have had some experience of interviews with hostile Government officials, and I can so well understand what she meant when she wrote of holding on to that speck of blue sky.

Her personality must have made an impression even on Lecour, for before she left he gave her *carte blanche* to go over the women's prison at St. Lazare, on the order for which he wrote in his own hand a sentence desiring " that every facility should be given to the very honourable lady from England "; but he flared up in anger when she mentioned a particular girl who was then being tormented by the Paris Police and with sudden irritation burst out : " Mais quelles bêtises vous ont-elles dit." (*Personal Reminiscences of a Great Crusade.*)

Of her Paris visit she wrote to her sister : " I must tell you when we meet of some of the persons in Paris in whose mind a change was wrought. At night after my long days of calling from house to house was over, people would come creeping up my lodging stairs to say a few words to apologise for never having seen clearly before, and sometimes to say they were too uneasy to sleep after what I had said." The addresses given by Mrs. Butler on this tour were printed as a pamphlet *Une Voix dans le Desert*, and the history of this first tour and the subsequent work of the Federation in France and Switzerland, Germany

*See Life of George Butler. By Josephine E. Butler.

and Italy is described at length in a book : " The New Abolitionists," published in 1876. The following passage from a letter to her dearly loved sister, Madame Meuricoffre, describes the work she was undertaking during this Continental visit :

" I live over again in thought the sweet days I spent with you. I look back upon that time as something sacred ; but it leaves a blank in my heart. I realise more than before what a loss it is to us to be so far and so long separated, and I feel more than ever the tenacity of early affection, and the ties of kindred. Ah ! how often I lie awake at night thinking of those hours we spent together. It was a sunshine and happiness to prepare me for the hard work which was to follow ; a suffering piece of work, though full of interest and hope. Going from city to city, tired and weary, always to meet with sharp opposition and cynicism, and ever new proofs of the vast and hideous oppression, is like running one's breast upon knife points, always beginning afresh before the last wound is healed. You understand, don't you ? I utter this little cry to you, but I am not despondent. This is really only physical weakness, I think, for I have to praise God for good work accomplished, and for souls inspired to work."

Lyons, Marseilles, Genoa, Geneva, Florence, Naples, Rome, Turin, Neuchâtel, Chaux-de-Fonds and Lausanne were visited during this tour, and wherever Mrs. Butler went she found men and women ready to catch the fire of her own inspiration, though, on the Continent as in England, she found " many professing Christians " in love with

legalized vice. " What a searcher of secret motives,
what a discoverer of the thoughts and intents of
the heart is this question of ours !" she writes,
" Think of your poor little curly French dandy,
of whom you expected no seriousness, showing
such a true insight and clear moral sense, and
going straight to the root of the matter, and then
of these " deeply religious " and immaculately
virtuous men who become pale with rage when
they foresee a danger of their sons being deprived
of " sanitary protection " in their " vices." Victor
Hugo had already written to her in 1870, on the
appearance of the Ladies' Manifesto against the
C. D. Acts. " I am with you, Madame and ladies,
I am with you to the fullest extent of my power.
All noble hearts and lofty spirits will be on your
side." She realised, on this visit, that his words
had been prophetic, for wherever she went men
and women of the noblest character responded to
her challenge.

The following quotation, taken from a report
of a Swiss Meeting by Professor Sheldon Amos,
emphasises the difficulties of fighting a system that
is not based on law but on police administration
only :

" There is one great difference between the
English and the Continental modes of viewing
laws affecting prostitution; namely, that in
most Continental countries, including Switzerland, large and indefinite powers are understood to belong to the police, in dealing with
this as with other matters; while in England
the far greater regard for individual liberty
causes the powers of the police to be more

strictly limited and defined. It is quite possible on the Continent for a whole system of registration and of *Maisons Tolérées* to be introduced at the mere discretion of the police, without any law being made on the subject at all, or even in the face of a prohibitory statute."

When Mrs. Butler returned to London she reported the results of her mission to a large gathering of British Abolitionists and it was decided to form an International Abolitionist Society. This, the first International Association for Moral Reform, was founded at a meeting in Liverpool on March 19th, 1875, under the title of " The British, Continental and General Federation for the Abolition of Government Regulation of Prostitution." Mrs. Butler was elected honorary secretary of the Federation. It contained such men and women as Yves Guyot, Madame Avril de Sainte Croix, Aimé Humbert, Guiseppe Nathan, Monsieur and Madame de Morsier, Alfred de Meuron, Henri Pierson, Professor Hornung, E. De Préssensé, T. Monod, Emile de Laveleye, and many others ; but on the Continent as in England, it was Josephine Butler who led and inspired the struggle. To Continental Abolitionists as to her English colleagues, then and now, " her name," as Madame Avril de Sainte Croix has finely said : " is a banner."

Thus was founded, in large part through the work of Josephine Butler, one of the earliest of the unofficial international Societies for social and legal reform which have been such an important feature of the practical progress of the last fifty years.

Josephine Butler

It is perhaps not sufficiently remembered what an important part women have taken in the last hundred years in the creation of the idea of international organisations for political and social ends. Mrs. Butler did not originate this idea, but she eagerly adopted it and expanded and emphasised as no one else had done.

Everyone knows about the American women who came over to London in 1840 to take part in an International Anti-Slavery Congress, and how they were not allowed to take their seats by their more hidebound British colleagues ; moreover, that William Lloyd Garrison, easily first among the American opponents of slavery, declined to take his seat when informed that the women had been excluded. He with characteristic humour said he " preferred to join the ladies." American Suffragists believe that this slight to the women delegates gave the first great impulse in the U.S.A. to the political enfranchisement of Women. Among other international organisations mention should be made of the World's Women's Christian Temperance Union, founded in 1853, and worked by American women on international lines ; also the International Council of Women founded by the Marchioness of Aberdeen and Temair in 1870 ; and the International Women's Suffrage Alliance with its splendid President, Mrs. Chapman Catt, which came into existence a few years later. These women's international Societies educated their members, drawn from 36 to 40 different countries, to discuss controversial political subjects with tact, humour and good temper, and were successful in very greatly furthering the objects they had in view. In my opinion they also materially contributed, by their example and by the spirit they had diffused, to the successful launching of the League of Nations in Paris in 1919.

Several of Mrs. Butler's more active associates became so blinded by the heat and dust of the conflict as to be unable to perceive the great progress which her cause had already made, and still more unable to realise the approach of important victories in the near future. But this attitude of mind was not shared by Mrs. Butler. As Professor Stuart wrote of her after her death, she was nearly always calmly confident of the success of the principles for which she contended : " Her industry and application were unbounded. She was very full of humour and while deeply in earnest had the faculty of being at times charmingly gay."

And things were working out favourably to the spread of Mrs. Butler's views even in Paris. In the late autumn of 1876 a newspaper war suddenly broke out in France kindled by the numerous cases of arbitrary and cruel action on the part of the *Police des Moeurs*, and frequent arrests both of men and women for resisting, and even for speaking against this force. As a result the Paris Municipal Council, which was opposed to the system, appointed a commission of enquiry and invited certain persons from different countries who had studied the question to give evidence before it. Mr. and Mrs. Butler, Mr. Stansfeld and Professor Stuart were invited from England and went to Paris to give their evidence in January, 1877.

This naturally led directly to a very considerable extension of their knowledge of the friends and

THE RIGHT HON. JAMES STUART, M.P.

(From a copy of the unfinished portrait by H. Herkoner in the possession of the A.M.S.H.)

sympathisers with their cause in France and other continental countries. These they found in all classes, from working men and women who had an unrivalled knowledge of the C. D. system from the home-makers point of view, to distinguished jurists and journalists. This in its turn, with the new knowledge it brought, led to a great extension of the work of the International Abolitionist Federation, which held its first meeting in Geneva in September, 1877, and " from that time," as M. Yves Guyot said : " the Regulation System was doomed in Europe." This Congress drew up the Charter of the Federation. It was a grave and considered document divided under the heads of Hygiene, Morality, Social Economy, Law and Benevolence. The findings of the Committees on the foregoing subjects were accepted by the Congress and confirmed at subsequent meetings of the Federation. It is interesting to note that this Charter of the Federation not only governs the section of its various branches to this day, but that its provisions have in effect, formed the basis of modern International Medical pronouncements upon venereal Disease. From the time of the founding of the International movement, the title of " Repealers " was presumably altered to " Abolitionists," and this is the title by which Mrs. Butler's followers are known to-day.

The work in Switzerland, in spite of the fact that the headquarters of the Federation are at Geneva, has had many a serious setback. But the position now (in 1926) is more favourable than it has ever been before. In 1925 the tolerated houses had been closed and the Police des Mœurs abolished in every canton in Switzerland with one exception. This was the town of Geneva where the regulation system remained in force until November 30th, 1925. It is a happy coincidence that the last tolerated house there was closed in the same year that the Jubilee celebrations of the Federation (which was founded in Geneva in 1875) were held in that historic city. Those who took part in the celebrations at Geneva were confronted on every side by posters *protesting against the closing of these houses*. Nevertheless, they were closed, and, in spite of the efforts of a Committee formed to keep them open, and the presenting of a petition signed by 2,500 citizens asking the Conseil d'Etat to reconsider their decision, they are to remain closed. The Conseil d'Etat has decided that the Petition cannot be received, and that the decision to close the houses is irrevocable.*

It is interesting to note that an inquiry into the incidence of venereal disease was carried out in Switzerland from October, 1920, to September 30th, 1921, and the results were published in 1924. The figures for the three most populous towns, Zürich, Basle and Geneva are very instructive. The populations are as follows : Zürich 207,161 ; Basle 135,976 ; Geneva 135,059. Geneva although the third in the list in point of population, is at the top with regard to venereal disease, and Geneva was then the only town in Switzerland where regulation of prostitution was in force. The figures for Geneva showed 132·1 per 10,000 persons affected with disease, while for Basle the figures were 98·5

---

* For the legal arguments advanced for this decision by the Conseil d'Etat *see* Bulletin Abolitionniste Avril-Mai, 1926.

per 10,000, and Zürich 121·7 per 10,000. Further, only 55 per cent. of the doctors in Geneva answered the enquiry while 76 per cent. of the doctors in Zürich and 80 per cent. of the doctors in Basle replied. The Report, therefore, suggests that the real proportion of disease in Geneva is even higher than the figures show, thus giving a striking though not an isolated instance, of the complete failure of the regulation system to lower the incidence of disease.

In 1876 Mr. H. J. Wilson and the Rev. J. P. Gledstone went on a mission to the United States of America, where they found many friends and spent a very busy and useful time. An important and well documented manifesto was drawn up by the Federation and the National Medical Association of Great Britain and Ireland for the Abolition of State Regulation of Prostitution, criticising the American proposals to introduce Regulation and giving the history and results of such legislation in Europe and especially in England. It was addressed to members of the American legislature and to the Medical Profession in the United States. Mr. Wilson and Mr. Gledstone inaugurated some new Abolitionist Societies and encouraged those already in existence.

In July, 1886, a great meeting of the International Abolitionist Federation, attended by delegates from Europe and America, was held in London to celebrate the English victory and consolidate the attack on Regulation throughout the world. Mrs. Butler was unable, owing to the severe illness of her husband, to attend all the meetings of the Congress, but she was able to give the following address at Exeter Hall to a full meeting of delegates. It is so wise, so tolerant, so characteristic of her that it is given in full.

" We have learned deep lessons and great lessons in our long years of conflict, crowned by the victory to which our President has so kindly alluded—lessons of faith, not in ourselves, but in the power of truth. I am reminded, as I stand here, at the close, so to speak, of one chapter of the history of our cause and the opening of another, of the noble words of John Stuart Mill : ' Fear not,' he said ; ' fear not the reproach of Quixotism or of fanaticism ; but after you have well weighed what you undertake, and are convinced that you are right, go forward ; even though you do it at the risk of being torn to pieces by the very men through whose changed hearts your purpose will one day be accomplished.' That man, John Stuart Mill, had discernment to recognise what is the fountain-head of all true energy to bring about real reformation—namely the changed hearts of men.

" I am reminded, too, of the words of William Lloyd Garrison. " When the necessary revolution in the mind of the people is completed, that in the institutions of the country will follow, as day follows night. We are grateful to be permitted to assist in this magnificent event. The scorn of the world ; the anathemas of the Church ; the sacrifice of all worldly objects of ambition—may be well endured for the promotion of a cause, in the issues of which are involved the deliverance of the slave, the purification of the country, and the progress of the race."

" We stand this day between a victory gained —and the future of the Federation. From this vantage ground we look around over a prospect in regard to our future work which, it must be confessed, looks, at first sight, somewhat intricate and perplexing. The task before us is, first, as Garrison said, to produce the necessary revolution in the minds of the people—the people of the whole civilised world. In order to that end, and recognising the world-wide character of the evil to be attacked, we have banded ourselves together as a Federation. But, in practice, we do not find that the federal principle is always easy to maintain and to work. The differences of language, of national and social traditions, of the state of public opinion and of the laws—and, above all, the difference in status which woman has won for herself in the different nations banded together in the Federation— make it difficult to move along all together on a common line.

" This difficulty appears just where we take the first step beyond the central and immediate duty which we have set ourselves to fulfil, namely, the abolition of all State regulation of vice ; and it increases in proportion as we step beyond that central duty.

" We shall postpone the difficulties and inevitable differences of opinion among us, if we keep strictly to that central point ; and we have reason enough to do so. Though (as we have just heard), a progress, and a hope of

approaching victory, can be recorded here
and there ; yet what is the fact ? That system,
with all its tyranny and horror, and its corrupt-
ing influences over society at large, exists in
almost every capital in Europe and in our
Colonies and Dependencies. Shall I, then,
call you again to rally your forces around
that centre ? For our work in that respect
is only beginning, and is not done. I do not
say that it is our only aim—our ultimate aim—
as citizens and as lovers of humanity. Far
from it. I speak for myself—and, I believe,
for a large majority of my colleagues—when
I say that our aim is to purify society by doing
battle with that which Victor Hugo calls " the
slavery of modern times—not yet abolished—
prostitution itself."

" It is needless to reiterate here the arguments
by which we have proved a hundred times that
by attacking the attitude of Governments
towards prostitution we are making the most
public appeal which it is possible to make to
the conscience of society—of mankind—on
this subject. And this public attack is essential
in order to produce the revolution in public
opinion just alluded to ; and which would
never have been promoted to the same extent
by private advice and domestic teaching, or
any more quiet and less aggressive methods.
It has already been urged—and I think the
advice is excellent—that in everything which
goes beyond the mere abolition of the system
of regulation, every national group or section
of workers throughout the world should act

with perfect freedom ; that there should be no attempt at centralisation or uniformity here ; that experiments should be tried, in the regions of preventive and rescue work ; in legislation if need be ; and in all kinds of individual and organised action—against the monster Social Vice. We must not seek to control each other, or judge each other in too critical a spirit— much less censure and denounce every case of attempted action for good which does not wholly agree with our own ideas. The greatest latitude and elasticity should be permitted, so long as the central principle of our League is not invaded. Then alone will a solemn protest be called for.

" I, as a woman, speaking for all women, declare that I shall continue to apply it with implacable sternness to every proposition, whether in the direction of hygienic or legislative measures, to any State interference for the external repression of feminine immorality.

" I said that in facing the future we find ourselves confronted by many perplexities and difficulties. I do not now speak of central principles ; but of the organisation and practical administration of the Federation, in the maintenance of our daily warfare. In this region I do not myself greatly desire uniformity. There is a danger often of sacrificing unity of spirit to a strained attempt at uniformity. I had rather see the genius of each nation develop itself freely in its organised methods. People must have their mistakes ; and, if necessary, retrace their steps and do better the second time.

Yet in this region, no doubt, some degree of centralisation may seem to be needful. That will be a matter for sectional discussion.

" While speaking of organisation, will you suffer me to sound a note of warning ? In my own life's experience I have frequently seen that *life*, living power, is sacrificed to the perfecting of organisation. You may perfect your organisation to the utmost ; but if not filled and permeated with life, it will not bring about a single real reform, nor bring you a step nearer to the " necessary revolution "— the changed hearts of men, which John Stuart Mill speaks of. It is a well-constructed altar upon which the fuel is neatly laid ; but it is not kindled into a glow except by the living spark applied to it, nor kept to a uniform heat except by a living breath perpetually fanning it. I have almost a dread of organisation. People are apt to become too busy and absorbed with it ; and when they succeed in getting it into beautiful working order they contemplate it with satisfaction, and are tempted to conclude that it must be doing a good work ; while sometimes it is doing nothing vital or aggressive.

" Someone has lately spoken of the Apostolic order in the evolution of a great reform. First He gave them apostles and prophets ; afterwards teachers and evangelists. Let us be sure that we are not in any of our national sections working fruitlessly in a reversed order ; beginning, so to speak, at the wrong end ; overestimating the utility of machinery ; and forgetting a little the essential thing, the power of the unseen Spirit, which bloweth where it listeth ; like the wind of heaven, which you cannot bind, or drill, or regulate ; but whose nature is such that, beginning as the softest summer breeze in some remote glade, it becomes the rushing mighty wind, sweeping through the whole earth, resistless, all-purifying.

" Seek men and women first—before any machinery. If you have not got them, seek the breath of that wind which will breathe upon the dry bones, and make them live and spring to their feet. Then let them fall into their places and ranks in our army. Then comes the time for drill ; but it is of no use to drill marionettes.

" When the era of teachers and evangelists arrives, then organisation becomes a necessity. Order, the law of God's universe, must be applied. But do, dear friends, beware of thinking that organisation is the first and most important thing. Beware of thinking that good statutes, rules, a sound financial basis, a regular income—are needful, before you can make any effectual attack on an enemy which is daily and hourly—at this very hour—murdering souls and bodies.

" Our Father in heaven knoweth that we have need of material resources ; and He will justify the faith that steps boldly forth, long before all these things are seen visibly to exist.

Although Mrs. Butler died in 1906, before the full results of the work on the Continent had become apparent, she knew that there could now be no turning back for the Abolitionist movement. Medical and scientific knowledge, facts and figures were beginning to range themselves on the side of liberty and justice. Expediency defeated its own ends and left its supporters without evidence or justification. The last chapter of this book will give proofs of the world-wide growth and acceptance of Abolitionist ideas and show how faithfully and truly she laboured, and the abundance and splendour of the harvest.

CHAPTER XI.

THE ATTACK ON REGULATION IN INDIA AND THE COLONIES.

"We have become deeply convinced in our long warfare that we need not only the mighty impulse of love in the heart, but also light in the brain ; we need to rally all the forces of our understanding and intellect, and to bring to a focus all the inventive power with which God may have endowed us ; and there is nothing which quickens the inventive faculty as to ways and means, so much as a horror of some deep injustice done, and the desire to defeat that injustice and to save its victims."—JOSEPHINE BUTLER.

THE story of the Campaign against the C. D. Acts in India, is in its essence the story of the fight against Regulation everywhere. When victory was won in this country in 1886, Mrs. Butler saw clearly that belief in the system was by no means dead and that many believers in Regulation had bowed to a storm of popular indignation without conviction in their hearts that the whole system was both wrong and useless.

She knew too much of the power and scope of the Regulationist movement which was world-wide in character to under-rate its influence, and she was always convinced that women must from the nature of the conflict, be foremost in opposing it. She says on this point :

" My mind had been long troubled by the thought of the growing and gigantic nature of the Abolitionist work in the various countries of the world, and of the need and lack of women workers. I knew that women must always continue to be at the heart and in the fore-front of the work in order to ensure success.

A woman moveover, who enters this war, must, while hating injustice, impurity, and tyranny with a perfect hatred, be free from personal bitterness against men—against any man."

She believed that constant watchfulness was necessary even in England : she therefore urged the Ladies' National Association in the moment of victory to remain ready for work. The National Association with the various other bodies formed to obtain repeal of the C. D. Acts had been dis-solved in 1886, but a nucleus remained in being and later became the British Branch of the Inter-national Abolitionist Federation, and with the Ladies' National Association,* working as always in close co-operation and under the leadership of Mrs. Butler, fought the battle of repeal throughout the British Empire.

In 1858 the British Government had taken over the control of Indian affairs which had hitherto been administered by the East India Company. Regulation had been in force in India for certain regiments and in an irregular fashion even prior to 1858. In 1859 a Royal Commission was appointed to enquire into the Sanitary State of the Army in India, and in 1864 an attempt was

---

* In 1915 these two Societies amalgamated under the title of The Association for Moral and Social Hygiene, which thus carries on in direct succession the work Mrs. Butler began.

made under Government Regulations, supplemented in 1868 by the Contagious Diseases Act, to put all the various irregular attempts on a definite footing. The C. D. Acts in India were not applied, of course, to the native civil population except when they were used for the purpose of providing native women for the men of British regiments stationed in India. Regulation of prostitution in India, therefore, was dealt with under Special Cantonment Acts.* Their purpose is expressly stated in the following extract known as the "Infamous Memorandum,"issued by Major-General Chapman, under instructions from the Commander-in-Chief, in 1886 the very year it will be noted in which the C. D. Acts were finally repealed in Great Britain :

> " To arrange for the effective inspection of prostitutes attached to regimental bazaars, whether in cantonments or on the line of march."

> " To have a sufficient number of women, to take care that they are sufficiently attractive, to provide them with proper houses."

The " Memorandum " includes references to many previous instructions on the subject, amongst which it is pointed out that " the number of women on the register is not in proportion to the number of men who visit them." Also that " His Excellency will be prepared to sanction any reasonable expenditure from cantonment funds on the measures therein suggested."

* *See* Mayne " Cantonment Law compared with the General Law in India," 1899, *also* " The History of a Sanitary Failure," by H. J. Wilson, M.P., 1898.

The existence of this Memorandum was not known in this country until 1888.

The Abolitionists immediately took up the challenge. Meetings and Conferences were held, statistics collected and circulated, constant Parliamentary vigilance was maintained by a group of friendly members of Parliament led by Mr. H. J. Wilson, M.P., and Professor Stuart, M.P. The Indian C. D. Acts were repealed in 1888 as the result of public indignation, but Abolitionists in this country were convinced that their abolition was only in name and not in fact. Mrs. Butler writing in " The Present Aspect of the Abolitionist Cause in India," says :

" Rumours which had been continually reaching us since 1888, forced us to the conclusion that the Indian authorities were not obeying the Resolution of the House of Commons, and weight was given to this conclusion by two facts : first, that the new Cantonments Act gave such powers as permitted easily the restoring and working of the system ; and second, that the most prominent Anglo-Indian journals triumphantly declared that they intended to outwit us, and could render nugatory the injunctions sent from home. Mr. Alfred Dyer, of Bombay, by his persistence in discovering and forwarding home the facts and documents providing for the continuance of the system, has won for himself the honour of being cordially hated by the Anglo-Indian military authorities."

This opinion was confirmed by the attitude of Anglo-Indian newspapers from which the following quotations are taken :

" Government," said one, " is to be congratu-
lated on the step it has taken to check the
further spread of this terrible scourge, while
keeping its remedial efforts well within the
limitations prescribed by the House of Commons " . . . " It requires no keen insight into
the motives which influence the human mind
to discover how readily a resident of the kind
indicated would yield ungrudging obedience
to any injunctions which it might please the
Commanding Officer to impose as a consideration for the postponement of what might
otherwise be an immediate sentence of expul-
sion. Such in its essential features is the scheme
the Government has indirectly, we had almost
said covertly, formulated for dealing with this
crying evil."

Another paper is still more frank :

" The religious fanatics who howled until a
weak Government gave way to their clamour
. . . will probably howl again now at the way
the old order of things will be enforced under
another name, but with very little difference
in manner . . . The way the Indian Government have got over the difficulty is simply
by classing venereal diseases in the same cate-
gory as small-pox and other contagious diseases
which the law provides for by segregation,
special hospitals, etc., so that really the authorities have turned Dyer and Co.'s flank and the
soldier will no longer be the victim of a
dangerous experiment."

Yet another, " The Medical Record," says of
the new rules:

" Their phraseology is the work of a master in the art of making a thing look as unlike itself as it well can be."

Two American women, Mrs. Elizabeth Andrews and Dr. Katherine Bushnell, who were on a visit to this country, came under the influence of Mrs. Butler, and they volunteered to go out to India and make a report on actual conditions in the Cantonments. This they did in circumstances of great difficulty, with the utmost courage and resource. Their report confirmed the worst fears of the Abolitionists in Great Britain. A great Campaign of protest was carried on in Parliament and throughout the country with the result that the Cantonments Acts were again amended in 1895. Dr. Bushnell and Mrs. Andrews published their impression of their Indian Tour in 1898, in a book called " The Queen's Daughters in India," dedicated to Mrs. Butler.

Abolitionists found a strong body of opinion in this country in favour of Regulation in India because of the peculiar difficulties by which regiments sent out from this country were surrounded. The majority of the soldiers were unmarried, they were cut off from their own country-women, they found themselves in a strange land, and in a climate peculiarly trying to Englishmen. People who would have been ready perhaps, to protest against any form of Regulation in this country were willing to support it in India for the sake of the soldiers, and the supposed gain to their health. A Committee of women was formed, under Government auspices, which advocated a type of Regulation in India even more drastic than the

Government plan. But their arguments had no solid
foundation. They were founded on expediency.
The Abolitionist arguments concerning the futility
of Regulation were found to be as apt to Indian as
to European conditions, for they were inspired by
principles which are of permanent and universal
application, and as such they were unaffected by
difference of climatic or social conditions.

In addition Abolitionists urged on the Government a greater concern for the mental and physical
welfare of the soldier in India, the provision of
facilities for games and other kinds of recreation
and study, and the provision of better and more
sanitary regimental quarters.

The final repeal of the Contagious Diseases Acts
in India, which Mrs. Butler, alas, did not live to see,
was accomplished by campaigns carried on in India
by the Rev. T. and Mrs. Katherine Dixon supported
by funds and information from the British Society,*
who were at the same time rousing public opinion
in the country, and bringing pressure to bear on
the Government at home. Mrs. Dixon was working
in India during the war, 1914-18, speaking all
over the country to men and women, civilians and
soldiers, with the result that a strong public
opinion against Regulation was aroused and it
was abolished. Mrs. Dixon, like Mrs. Andrews,
Dr. Bushnell, and Mr. Dyer, worked under the
inspiration of Mrs. Butler.

In Hong Kong, Singapore, Ceylon, Gibraltar,
Malta, South Africa and Australia, the Abolitionists
were also at work opposing principle to expediency
and challenging on every side the overt assumption

* The Association for Moral and Social Hygiene.

that prostitution is a necessity and must be regulated. Mrs. Butler did not live to see how completely her challenge has been justified. Except in Great Britain, the main harvest of her sowing was reaped after her death.

CHAPTER XII.

Josephine Butler's Enduring Influence.

"We are of those who represent the imperishableness of principles, one of the many assurances of immortality. And the conviction deepens in us from year to year that the soul of a people can be appreciably lifted up by the steadfast pressure of an eternal principle, that 'righteousness is the only power which will finally compel submission, and that one—with God—is always a majority.' Let us be of good courage then." —Josephine Butler.

THE supporters of the C. D. Acts in Great Britain had been very lavish in their confident prophecies that repeal would be followed by a great and terrible increase of the diseases they purported to combat. The exact reverse was what really happened. No one, of course, was so foolish as to suppose that these diseases would miraculously disappear because a wrong method of dealing with them had been abandoned. But the whole subject was thenceforth approached in a calmer and more rational spirit. It will be remembered that evidence had been given before the Royal Commission of 1871 by opponents of the C. D. Acts, recommending an ample supply of free clinics all over the country for dispensary treatment, with no compulsory powers and no disclosure of the names of the patients; and it was stated by one of the witnesses that such a plan had been adopted and had had good results in Sweden. But the Commission of 1871, gave no recommendation for the adoption of this system. Forty years later, however, it began to be plain, even in official circles, that this was a reasonable, and unobjectionable method of dealing with the evil and we find in the Report on Venereal Diseases by Dr. R. W. Johnstone, Medical Officer of the Local Government Board, published in 1913 : the following passage :—

"It cannot be too strongly urged that the best method of controlling venereal disease and protecting the innocent from infection would be *the provision of means for early and accurate diagnosis, with skilled advice and adequate treatment available for all infected persons.* In short, the essence of the problem is how to get a willing patient at the earliest time to the doctor from whom, or to the institution from which, such advice and treatment is to be had."

Again when the Commission of 1913* was appointed, the whole atmosphere in which these problems were dealt with had changed ; and what had been rejected almost without argument in 1871 became the chief constructive feature of the Report issued more than forty years later. In this we see the result of the continuous Campaign initiated by Josephine Butler and continually growing in strength as knowledge on the subject increased.

In 1913 there was no repetition in the Press of the wild hysterical attacks on those who opposed the policy of the Acts. The terms of reference

* The Royal Commission on Venereal Diseases. 1913.

were : *To enquire into the prevalence of venereal
diseases in the United Kingdom, their effects upon
the health of the community, and the means by which
those effects can be alleviated or prevented, it being
understood that no return to the policy or provisions
of the C. D. Acts of 1864, 1866 or 1869 is to be
regarded as falling within the scope of the enquiry.* In
1913 three women were placed among the fifteen
Commissioners.* Although precluded from considering the policy of the C. D. Acts, the Commission in the final report placed on record their
view based on the evidence they had received
from several continental experts that "*no advantage
would accrue from a return to the system of these
Acts. So far from this being the case it is to be noted
that the great improvement as regards venereal
diseases in the Navy and Army has taken place
since the repeal of the Acts.†*"
One of the tables included in the Report of
the Commission of 1913 attracted much notice
and comment. It is as follows :
"Social Distribution.—The following table
gives the recorded death-rate per million from
syphilis and the three consequential diseases
of males above 15, distributed among eight
classified groups of the population :

* I was invited by Lord Morley, in a very polite letter, to be one
of these, but I felt compelled to decline the invitation because I was
at that moment (August, 1913) at the very height of my suffrage work ;
I had put my hand to that plough and could never look back ; and I
felt that I could not materially add to my work. But I ventured to
suggest the name of Dr. Helen Wilson as a very suitable member of
the Commission. The suggestion was, however, disregarded.—M. G. F.

† For details *see* Appendix, Summary of Report of the Commission
of 1913.

Class.	Social Status or Occupation.	Death-rate per million.
1.	Upper and middle	302
2.	Intermediate, between 1 and 3 ...	280
3.	Skilled labour	264
4.	Intermediate, between 3 and 5 ...	304
5.	Unskilled labour	429
6.	Textile workers	186
7.	Miners	177
8.	Agricultural labourers	108

The arguments in support of the C. D. Acts have been in fact totally shattered by experience as the following figures show :

" When the Acts were suspended in 1883 the figures for V. D. in the Home Army were 260 cases per 1,000 men. When the Acts had been first put in force in 1864 the ratio was 261 per 1,000. Thus after 20 years of Regulation there was practically no diminution of disease in the Army. It was not until the whole Regulation System was finally abolished in 1886 that venereal diseases showed a steady and continuous decline, only broken by the South African War. Whereas the usual ratio in the Regulation Period fluctuated round about 240 per thousand, the average ratio for recent years is less than 60 per thousand and although the usual official figures have not been published for the war years we believe we are correct in saying that the average venereal rates for the Army in Great Britain during the years 1914-1919 were less than 40 per 1,000 men."

But it is not only in Great Britain that the Abolitionist propaganda has been justified. The results are the same everywhere. Compare, for example, the following extracts from Memorandum No. 04745—1 (A—G 5), addressed by the Adjutant-General in India to General Officers Commanding, Divisions and Brigades, dated August 2, 1918, with the " Infamous Memorandum " quoted in Chapter XI.

". . . It is reported, that in certain units, officers have even suggested to their men, that if they find continence difficult, they should resort only to certain named houses where precautions are enforced ; and it is also stated that lectures, delivered by medical officers and others with the object of warning men of the consequences of disease, conclude by advising continence, but suggesting that, if temptation be too strong, men should visit only such places as are under so-called medical control. Not only is such advice contrary to orders, not only does it offer direct temptation but it offers it *under guarantees which are quite illusory ;* since according to the most recent expert medical opinion and research there can be no system of examination which can justify any guarantees of immunity from disease."

" Section 179, Cantonment Code, lays down that the Cantonment Authority has the power to close down any brothel. The wording of this Section, has, in the past, led to an erroneous impression that houses that are not prohibited are necessarily under medical supervision and therefore safe.

" It has, however, now been ruled that it is doubtful if Section 179, Cantonment Code, really confers the necessary powers for the closing down of all brothels, and therefore, the Governor-General in Council issued a rule under the Defence of India (Consolidation) Rules, 1915, authorising the Competent Military Authority to close any brothel in Cantonments or the vicinity. This rule was published in Gazette of India notification No. 1636, dated 20th July, 1918, and a copy is attached for ready reference.

"As regards cantonments, the Commander-in-Chief directs that this order is to be generally applied, but discretion must be exercised when considering its application to places in the vicinity of Cantonments or Camps ; in these cases it will usually be advisable to consult the civil authorities. He also wishes Commanding Officers to explain to the men the reasons for these rules. If this is done, there can be no misapprehension of the fact that immorality is in no way recognised or tolerated officially or unofficially. The excuse that certain houses were believed to be under State control will not be accepted."

The foregoing is an official letter ; it is the official recognition of the futility of regulation even in the difficult conditions created by large bodies of men, the majority of whom are celibate, quartered in a foreign land under trying climatic conditions.

If we want to appreciate the effect of Mrs. Butler's work and life we have only to compare the letter quoted on a previous page, in which a general officer orders women " for the use of the troops " on their arrival in a new camp. A very different spirit is to be found now as may be illustrated by letters written by young officers serving in India in the early part of the war of 1914-18.

My first extract is taken from an article by Dr. Jane Walker in *The Englishwoman* magazine of July, 1918, and describes what a young officer himself saw while in India. He had been serving since 1914, and he wrote in 1917 : " The men come back after two or more years in Mesopotamia and camp life and are stuck down in another large camp in the middle of India with *nothing to do and nowhere to go*.* They have got lots of money, and are longing to enjoy themselves and have some fun, and to forget the war and its miseries. Instead of which, last year (1916) the Army authorities made absolutely no preparations for them, dumped them down in hundreds, often even without tents, told them to spend their month's holiday in that place, and ' if you want women, don't go to the bazaar ; such and such houses are all right.' Result : 9,000 out of 21,000 troops had to be left behind in hospital when their furlough was over, suffering from venereal disease."

It was left to the writer of the foregoing letter and others to open canteens and cinemas and organise games and amusements for the men so as to give them as jolly a time as possible and help to keep them out of mischief.

Look, too, at this extract from a letter from another young officer, since, alas ! killed.

* Italics are ours.—M. G. F. and E. M. T.

The Life and Work of

" The system of having inspected prostitutes
out here (India) continues. The only change
effected by the C. D. Acts agitation, so far as I
can gather, is that whereas the system used to
be open and officially sanctioned, it is now secret
and unofficially sanctioned. The day after we
arrived here, my Colour-Sergeant asked me to
speak to the men about it, as there were *authorised
women provided by the authorities*, which greatly
scandalised him. ' I don't believe,' he said, ' that
however much they like to inspect 'em they can
be sure that it's all right.' And, indeed, they can't,
for our regiment left numbers of men behind who
were too bad to be taken to Europe. It is a crying
shame and a foul disgrace to men who can treat
women so. It is the essence of slavery. I never
felt more ashamed of my sex than when I had to
speak to my Company about it. I felt bound to
defend the system as best I could, putting
on it an interpretation which I fear it does not
deserve, but I told them my own views and
wishes, and for the moment I knew they were
with me."

The letter of the Adjutant-General* in India
has been strongly reinforced in 1925 by the
publication of the Report of the Advisory Committee on Singapore set up by the Colonial Office.†
The Singapore administration was seeking from
the Government permission to set up a very severe
system of Regulation in order to deal effectively,
as it was hoped, with venereal disease in that
port. The Colonial Office referred the matter to

See page 137.
† First Report of the Advisory Committee on Social Hygiene. Cmd.
2501. 1925.

an Advisory Committee which, after prolonged
consideration of all the facts issued a unanimous
Report condemning the proposals. This Report,
from which the following extracts are quoted,
might in fact have been written by an Abolitionist
and it is not too much to say that it is the direct
result of Josphine Butler's life work.

" The draft Ordinance proposed to deal with
the situation by a far-reaching system of State
Regulation, including the licensing and medical
examination of all prostitutes. This system
is too well known to need any detailed description. The principal respect in which the
Singapore proposal differs from other systems
of the same kind, which have been tried in
different parts of the world, lay in the defini-
tion of the word ' prostitute,' a matter to
which we refer later.

" We would point out that it is proposed to
deal with the problem at Singapore by methods
which have been abandoned long ago, in this
country and more recently in other countries,
after acute controversy. Any attempt to estab-
lish a system of State Regulation in Singapore
would revive these controversies and would be
certain to meet with serious public criticism
and even resentment. The risk of alienating
public opinion in this country and elsewhere
might have to be faced if there were any reasonable hope that the methods would be successful,
but *State Regulation wherever it has been put
to the test has been marked by its failure to provide
a remedy for the evils for which it was designed,*[*]

[*] The italics are ours.—M. G. F. and E. M. T.

and has now almost entirely lost the support of medical opinion.

" We do not propose to recapitulate the many objections to State Regulation from the moral point of view, but we may add, that as applied in European Countries, it has never been instrumental in promoting public order or decency. On the other hand, it has been one of the main contributory causes of the traffic in women. In this connection we may point out that the Advisory Committee on the Traffic in Women and Children, appointed by the League of Nations, has drawn attention in its report to the connection between State Regulation and organised procuration, and in their third report, issued in April, 1924, they published the replies which they received from a number of States on the subject of State Regulation. The evils of the system in relation to the traffic in women are emphatically commented on in countries like Belgium, Holland, Poland and Czecho-Slovakia.

" Experience in different countries has shown conclusively that the periodical examination of prostitutes is ineffective from the medical point of view for the following reasons : (*a*) it cannot be carried out with sufficient thoroughness ; (*b*) even if the examination were most thorough no prostitute can ever be safely declared free from gonorrhœa, (*c*) syphilis if definitely cured can be reacquired, if only rendered non-infective it is not possible to say when or whether infection may return ; (*d*) if the woman is absolutely healthy at the examination she may be infected shortly after and may infect many others before she can be detected ; (*e*) even if not diseased herself she may be the carrier of contagion from one man to another ; (*f*) wherever prostitutes are known to be subject to compulsory periodic examination there results in men a false sense of security which tends to encourage promiscuity and to spread disease."

The most striking recent corroboration of Josephine Butler's views comes from the League of Nations, which in 1923 appointed an Expert Committee to make an exhaustive inquiry into the Traffic in Women on a world-wide scale. That Report was published in February, 1927, and should have very far-reaching results. In 1880 Josephine Butler said of the Traffic : " When the daylight is fully come, the conscience of Europe will be aroused and this masterpiece of hell will be shattered for ever." Her words have re-echoed through the world ever since and now after forty-seven years, the " conscience of Europe " is roused at last. The world-wide investigations* of the League of Nations Committee have proved to the hilt her contention that " the licensed house is the market for this traffic—where there are no licensed houses the traffic does not exist." The knowledge spread by this Report ought to sweep Regulation out of Europe for ever.

The growing influence of Josephine Butler is now visible in many different parts of the world. It is ever attracting more and more attention

---

* *See* Report of the Special Body of Experts on Traffic in Women and Children, Part I. Geneva, 1927. C. 52. 1927. lv. C.T.F.E. Experts 55.

and appreciation in countries where it was once
regarded with contempt and impatience. As I
write, in the autumn of 1927, I hear of two writers
one from France, and one from Belgium, who
are spending several weeks in England in order to
acquaint themselves more thoroughly with the
circumstances of her life and the education which
helped to make her what she was, and rendered
her capable, by sheer moral strength, to lift up
the slaves, whether male or female, of a debased
moral standard and to give them a new outlook
in life.

In 1925 the International Abolitionist Federation celebrated its Jubilee at Geneva, and it had
the satisfaction of knowing that the moral, legal,
and medical bases of its protest against Regulation,
set forth in faith at Geneva, 1877, had been scienti-
fically accepted and approved ; and that their
proposals for widespread voluntary treatment of
diseases had been adopted with great success
in Great Britain and Holland, and (in varying
degrees) in other countries of the world. As the
result of fifty years of propaganda and effort by
the Federation, the tolerated houses and the
police des moeurs have been abolished in
Norway, Denmark, Holland, Bulgaria, Serbia,
Czecho-Slovakia, Poland, Germany and Switzerland—with the exception of Geneva, where the
tolerated houses were not finally closed until the end
of 1925. Even France has a *projet de loi* whereby
the licensed houses will be abolished in three
years. Above all there has been a complete change
in medical and public opinion on the efficacy of
Regulation. The investigations of Mr. Abraham

Flexner, of New York, and the statistics and information gathered over a long period of years in a variety of countries by the Federation itself, have at long last proved that every charge brought against this system by Abolitionists in the early days of the Movement has been amply justified. There has been a change too, in the public attitude towards morality, and the necessity for a single moral standard for men and women is beginning to be understood. In 1925, fifty years after the first International Congress at Geneva, the following resolution was adopted by the International Union against the Venereal Peril at its meeting in Paris at the Faculty of Medicine :

" Considérant que la réglementation de la prostitution n'a, à aucune époque, et en aucun pays permis de limiter les dégats causés par les affections vénériennes :
" Que d'autre part, elle est contraire à toute justice et à toute idée de morale sociale ;
" Le Conseil de direction recommande :
" 1. La suppression de la réglementation de la prostitution.
" 2. L'application de mésures visant la totalité de la population et s'inspirant, dans la plus large mésure, du principe de la liberté individuelle."

Again in Paris in 1923 the International Congress of Social Hygiene declared " La réglementation de la prostitution, inutile en fait, inique en droit et doit être abolie."

This is, in effect, the echo of Josephine Butler's inspired protest in 1869. In the fulness of time her faith has been justified. The Abolition of the C. D. Acts in Great Britain struck a blow at the Regulation system from which it never recovered and the steady pressure of Abolitionist propaganda inaugurated by Josephine Butler will result at last in its final and complete overthrow. No other woman in history has had such far-reaching influence, or effected so wide-spread a change in public opinion.

CHAPTER XIII.

*"The Human Society towards which it is our duty
to strive, will have within it no* human dregs. *The
Law which it will obey will be, in deed and truth,
Common Law embracing within its retaining, guiding
arms, every man and every woman, and will be administered with justice to all, but with especial forbearance and
tenderness to the poor, the weak and the friendless."*

*"I believe that a time is coming when it will be
apparent that the principle for which we are contending
—the unity of the moral law, and the equality of all
human souls before God—is the most* fruitful and
powerful revolutionising principle *which the world
has ever known, and that we shall achieve a victory
in the course of years, and through much tribulation,
which will make our present efforts seem trivial for the
attainment of so great an end."*—JOSEPHINE BUTLER.

THUS during the fifty-eight years that
have passed since Josephine Butler made
her first great public protest, the system
of Regulation, attacked on every side
by herself and her followers, has crumbled in
country after country, disowned and discredited
even by those who saw in it, at first, the only
bulwark against disease and disorder. May then
those who have carried on the work that Josephine
Butler only laid down with her life in 1906 feel
assured that victory was finally won in 1927 ? By
no means—Regulation of Prostitution in its old
vile form is discredited and dying, but the spirit
which gave it form is by no means dead. There
is always the danger that the old system may
be replaced by another, which will be Regulationist

in spirit if not in name. Josephine Butler was
aware of this danger. In 1898 she wrote an emphatic
warning against

> " certain legal enactments and police measures
> which, though they may not intend it to be
> so, inevitably lead to the restoration of some
> system based on the false principles which
> are at the root of all Regulation. There are
> always *the inequality between the sexes, the
> negation of personal rights, and tyrannous and
> almost irresponsible powers placed in the hands
> of the executive.*"

This is precisely what has happened. In
many European counties, and in the United States
of America, systems which attempt to deal with
the problem of prostitution have been set up
which are based on compulsory reformation for
women and compulsory treatment for diseased
persons. Such systems contain within themselves
the possibilities of reviving all the old evils of the
past. They are based on inequality and the acceptance of the double moral standard : the very
principles which Josephine Butler challenged.
Even when, as in the United States, very severe
laws for the suppression of prostitution are drafted
to apply equally to both sexes, in administration
they apply to women only ; and, generally speaking,
to the poorer and weaker section of women only.
Men are left untouched, as the American Appeal
Court, has ruled that a man cannot be proceeded
against for prostitution. The administration of
the laws in New York City is in the hands of a
special force of plain clothes police, and it results
in the direct encouragement of the double standard,

and of a corrupt police force, for it ignores almost as completely as the old Regulation system, the equal partnership of the man in the act of prostitution. It ignores too, the fact that the demand on the part of men creates the supply in the persons of women. Schemes of suppression, schemes for compulsory health measures for diseased persons are all doomed to failure because they ignore, or fail to deal with, fundamental causes. The facts and statistics collected by various authorities in different countries are already witness to that failure.* Such schemes are built on sand, they have the stamp of futility upon them, they are unequal and unjust, and that condemns them for " Nothing endures that is founded on injustice "

Abolitionists then must be for ever on the alert to challenge these systems wherever they appear and under whatever name they may masquerade—whether in the form of unjust laws for the police control of alleged prostitutes in the streets, or of special laws or compulsory measures applied in the name of health or morality. The Abolitionists creed can be summed up in their leader's own words :

" Injustice is immoral, oppression is immoral, the sacrifice of the interests of the weaker to the stronger is immoral, and all these immoralities are embodied in all systems of legalised prostitution, in whatever part of the world or under whatever title they exist."

Josephine Butler was a spiritual power whose

---

*See Some Points concerning the Medical Control of Venereal Diseases in Great Britain, 1925 ; Women's Courts in New York City, April, 1924, (Shield) Conference Papers. Graz, 1924.

influence was not bounded by the narrow span of her own life, or by the limits of her country. Her influence goes on and lives and grows. She was in fact, one of the very great people who leave the world better than they found it and whose influence is continually increasing as the truth of their message to mankind is more and more confirmed by experience.

In nothing did Mrs. Butler show her greatness more than in her success in gathering under her banner distinguished men of leading position in science, literature and statesmanship, not only in England, but in the United States and most European countries, such as Victor Hugo, Mazzini, Garibaldi, Emile de Laveleye of Belgium, Aimé Humbert, Professor of Jurisprudence in Neuchâtel, Arbraham Flexner and James Stuart ; these were among the many men of eminence who recognised her as their leader, and did much to make her movement truly international.

She had in a marked degree, the qualities necessary to a Leader : patience, insight into character, unswerving determination, courage, self-sacrifice, sufficient knowledge of political affairs to recognise when the right moment came for a move onwards. She had also an inexhaustible fund of independence of judgment, for she led, and was far indeed from simply taking up the popular cry of the moment ; a special instance of this is to be found in her sympathy with the cause of her own country during the South African War ; for the majority, probably the very large majority, of her followers on the subject which she had made particularly her own, took the opposite view.

Josephine Butler

Had she then, it may be asked, no faults?
After searching very carefully, I think I have
discovered one. Characteristically it is the one
with which Mary Magdalene was also charged
when she broke the precious box of spikenard
over the Saviour's feet. Mrs. Butler was recklessly
generous to those on whom the perverseness of
men's laws and also of men's lawlessness had
brought very low in the world's esteem. She
herself tells of one " Marion " a repentant Magdalen
whom she had brought as a guest, and an honoured
guest, into her own house in Liverpool; Marion
had been " seduced " when a mere child of 15,
by a man much above her in social status and
three times her age. After a few years he completely abandoned her, leaving her absolutely
penniless; and for a time she sank lower and
lower till Mrs. Butler discovered and rescued
her. She seems to have had in many ways a remarkable mind responding eagerly to the refined and
intellectual atmosphere which she found in Mrs.
Butler's house. In both intellect and heart she
was among the elect of the earth. But the hand
of death was upon her. It came to her on a sunny
day in March, and Mrs. Butler writes: "After
her death the poor Mother came to attend her
funeral . . . *I had filled Marion's coffin with camelias,
banking them up all around her* . . . dressed as a
bride for her Lord, she looked quite lovely."

What camelias cost in March in Liverpool,
I cannot say, but reading this did make me feel
rather like Judas, and like those who said : " To
what purpose is this waste? For the ointment
ought to have been sold for much and given to

the poor." This extravagance—which may after all have soothed the wounded hearts of the poor father and mother—represents to me the only fault I have discovered in Josephine Butler.

As the years rolled on and she gradually became an old woman many of her former sources of happiness were taken from her. Her husband died in 1890 and this necessarily took from her much of her joy in life. They had been all in all to each other and had had everything in common ; and he had been her strength and support all through her most arduous work. In the more material aspects of her loss, her home was broken up ; for first as a schoolmaster, and later as Canon of Winchester, their home was an appendage of his office, and becoming a widow rendered her homeless. As he lay dying this thought haunted him, and he said to his sons : " If I die you will all be scattered to the winds ; poor dears, no more pleasant home in Winchester." (" Life of G. B.," by J. E. B., p. 430.) The sons, of course, had their own occupations and professions, and she was more alone in her domestic life than ever she had been before.

There were compensations of course ; when her sons married and had children, her grandchildren were a great delight to her. And, above all other consolations, she had her work, especially the development of it which was taking place outside her own country. This was a constant source of interest and also of thankfulness to her.

Josephine Butler's last public act was the writing of letters either of greeting or farewell to many of those who had been her collaborators in the great work of her life. These letters are all on the side of inclusiveness and against narrowness of view. She did not wish, in her own words, to belong to " a clique of pious people with no width of view." " I have seen," she wrote, " many just men who gave lifelong labour to casting out the evil spirits of tyranny, oppression, and injustice : and of these, whatever their formula of belief may have been, the Judge of all the World will say : " Well done."

Death came to her as a friend. She had no long illness, but her physical strength gradually declined and she died peacefully in her sleep, at Wooler, in her beloved Northumberland, on December 30th, 1906; the anniversary of Wycliffe's death. Her body rests, in the churchyard of Kirk-newton, where many of her ancestors are also buried.

———

The seed which she has sown can never die.

Appendix.

APPENDIX.

Mrs. Butler was a ready writer, and a full list of the various leaflets and pamphlets she wrote is almost impossible as the majority are now out of print. The following list contains all her books and most of her larger pamphlets. Those marked * can still be obtained.

The Education and Employment of Women. London, 1868.

Memoir of John Grey of Dilston. Edinburgh, 1869.

Women's Work and Women's Culture. 1869.

An Appeal to the People of England on the Recognition and Superintendence of Prostitution by Governments. Nottingham, 1870.

On the Moral Reclaimability of Prostitutes. London, 1870.

Sursum Corda. Liverpool, 1871.

Address in Craigie Hall, Edinburgh. Manchester, 1871.

Address at Croydon. London, 1871.

Vox Populi. Liverpool, 1871.

The Constitution Violated. Edinburgh, 1871.

*The New Era.** Liverpool, 1872.

Letter on the subject of Mr. Bruce's Bill. Liverpool, 1872.

Some thoughts on the Present Aspect of the Crusade. Liverpool, 1874.

Letter to the L. N. A. Liverpool, 1875.

*Une Voix dans le Desert.** 1875. Translated into English, 1913.

*Hour before the Dawn.** London, 1876.

Catharine of Siena. London, 1878.

*Government by Police.** London, 1879.

Appendix.

Social Purity. London, 1879.
Life of J. F. Oberlin. London, 1882.
The Salvation Army in Switzerland.* London, 1883.
Dangers of Constructive Legislation in Matters of Purity.* Bristol, 1883. Reprinted, 1914.
The Principles of the Abolitionists. London, 1885.
The Work of the Federation. London, 1885.
Rebecca Jarrett. London, 1886.
Our Christianity tested by the Irish Question. London, 1887.
The Revival and Extension of the Abolitionist Cause. Winchester, 1887.
The Dawn. London, 1888-96. An Occasional Sketch of the Work of the British, Continental and General Abolitionist Federation.
Recollections of George Butler. Bristol, 1892.
St. Agnes. London, 1893.
The Present Aspect of the Abolitionist Cause in relation to British India. London, 1893.
The Lady of Shunem. London, 1894.
Two Letters of Earnest Appeal and Warning. London, 1895.
A Doomed Iniquity. London, 1896.
Personal Reminiscences of a Great Crusade.* London, 1896. Reprinted, 1913.
Truth Before Everything.* London, 1897.
The Storm-Bell. London, 1898-1900. (A monthly magazine, edited and almost entirely written by J.E.B.)
Prophets and Prophetesses. Newcastle, 1898.
Native Races and the War. London, 1900.
Silent Victories. London, 1900.
In Memoriam, Harriet Meuricoffre. London, 1901.

Index.

INDEX.

Index.

Index.

Index.

159

Index.

Index.

Index.

162

Index.

Index.